EDEXCEL A-LEVEL/AS RELIGIOUS S

PAPER 3 NEW TESTAMENT STU

AS/A-LEVEL YEAR 1 REVISION GUIDE

Published independently by Tinderspark Press
© Jonathan Rowe 2018

CONTENTS

ABOUT THIS BOOK

This book offers notes for teachers and students revising Edexcel AS or A-Level Year 1 Religious Studies, Paper 3 (New Testament Studies). It summarizes the 3 Study Guides which are already available and which greatly expand on the notes in this book.

The AS/A-Level Year 1 topics are:

1   Context of the New Testament

2   Texts and interpretation of the Person of Jesus

3   Interpreting the text and issues of relationship, purpose and authorship

Topics 4-6 cover the topics in Year 2 of the A-Level. There are 3 study guides detailing these and a second revision guide for them will follow:

4   Ways of interpreting the scripture

5   Texts and interpretation: the Kingdom of God, conflict, the death and resurrection of Jesus

6   Scientific and historical-critical challenges, ethical living and the works of scholars

Exemplar exam questions are adapted from the specimen papers available to the public on the Edexcel website. The author claims no insight into the content of the actual exam.

 Text that is marked like this is a quotation from the Bible. Candidates should use some of these quotations in their exam responses.

 Text that is marked like this describes an important episode from the New Testament. Candidates should refer to events in the Gospels to illustrate arguments.

 Text that is marked like this is reference to a key scholar. Candidates shuld link ideas to key scholars wherever possible

Text in this typeface and boxed represents the author's comments, observations and reflections. Such texts are not intended to guide candidates in writing exam answers.

1 CONTEXT OF THE NEW TESTAMENT

1.1 PROPHECY REGARDING THE MESSIAH

This topic looks at the history of the **line of King David** and the **Suffering Servant** in the Book of Isaiah; it links these to the New Testament, especially **Matthew's 'proof texts'** which show Jesus to be the Messiah and the concept of the **"Messianic Secret"** in Mark's Gospel. **Raymond Brown** and **Morna Hooker** are the key scholars here.

1.2 THE WORLD OF THE FIRST CENTURY

This topic looks at the importance of **Hellenism** (Greek culture) and the **Roman occupation** for the Jews of Palestine as well as the different **Jewish sect**s formed in response to these influences. There are no key scholars for this section but the ancient historian Flavius Josephus is the main source.

KEY TERMINOLOGY:

Birth Narrative: Account of the birth of Jesus found in **Matthew** and **Luke**

Davidic: Descended from **Kind David** (c. 1000 BCE)

Futurist: Interpreting prophecy so that it applies to a future event

Galilee: Region in northern Palestine where Jesus came from

Hellenism: Greek philosophy and culture

Judea: Region in southern Palestine including Bethlehem and Jerusalem

Messiah: Promised leader and liberator of the Jewish nation

Messianic Secret: Puzzling feature of **Mark's Gospel** where Jesus keeps his identity as Messiah secret

Palestine: Region in the Middle East, bordering the Eastern Mediterranean, north of Egypt and south of Syria

Preterist: Interpreting prophecy so that it applies to events happening in the prophet's own time

Proof-Text: A quotation from the Old Testament intended to prove Jesus is the Messiah

Prophecy: A statement inspired by God and revealing God's purposes

Servant Songs: Passages of prophecy in the Old Testament **Book of Isaiah** describing a servant of God who is persecuted and killed but then returned to life and rewarded

1.1 PROPHECY REGARDING THE MESSIAH

A **PROPHECY** is a message inspired by God. This means it is a form of **revelation**. A person who passes on prophecies is a **PROPHET**.

- **PRETERIST** interpretation: Old Testament prophets are talking about their own time, offering warnings and advice from God

- **FUTURIST** interpretation: prophets are talking about Jesus as the future Saviour

> *For to us a child is born, to us a son is given, and the government will be on his shoulders. And he will be called Wonderful Counselor, Mighty God, Everlasting Father, Prince of Peace* **- Isaiah 9: 6**

Preterist = birth of a royal baby around 700 BCE

Futurist = birth of Jesus (700 years later) or the End of the World (**Apocalypse**)

MESSIAH means "*the anointed one*," or "*the chosen one.*" Originally meaning *anyone* who had been anointed to be God's chosen leader - it started to mean a *particular* person who was chosen by God for a very special destiny.

Christos (Christ) is the Greek word for **Messiah**.

- **THE KINGLY MESSIAH:** a king of the **line of David** who would defeat the Roman Empire and rule fairly and wisely

- **THE PRIESTLY MESSIAH:** a religious leader who would reform the priesthood, setting up a better, holier form of worship that was accessible to everyone.

- **THE PROPHETIC MESSIAH:** A great prophet who would guide the Jewish nation back to God in these troubled times.

- **THE SUFFERING MESSIAH**: A sacrificial victim who dies an atoning death (a death which makes up for other people's sins).

> *He will judge between the nations and will settle disputes for many peoples. They will beat their swords into plowshares and their spears into pruning hooks. Nation will not take up sword against nation, nor will they train for war anymore* **- Isaiah 2: 4**

1.1 THE IMPORTANCE OF THE LINE OF DAVID

The **Messiah** must be descended from the greatest King of Israel: **David**.

David: lived around 1000 BCE; began life as a humble shepherd boy from Bethlehem; led a rebellion against the cruel King Saul; founded the United Kingdom of **Israel**; ruled over a 'Golden Age' of just rule and pure religion; later his rule was tainted by his selfishness and family divisions.

Divided Monarchy: northern kingdom of **Israel** lasted until, in 722 BC; southern kingdom of **Judah** ruled for by **'the House of David'**, a line of kings descended from David; in 597 BCE, the Babylonians laid siege to Jerusalem, destroyed the city and its Temple and took the citizens away as prisoners of war.

Later, the Jews were ruled by other dynasties (eg **Herod**): many hoped for a *real* king of the Jews who would be a descendant of David because God had promised the Davidic line would not be ended

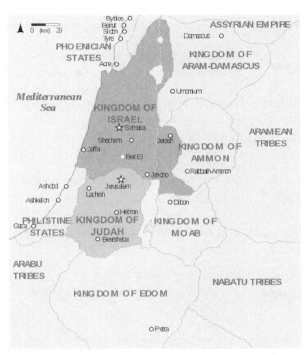

The Kingdoms of Israel and Judah in the 10th century BCE

Your house and your kingdom will endure forever before me; your throne will be established forever – **2 Samuel 7: 16**

What was needed for the 'Son of David' to appear? Jews had differing answers to this:

- **Religious Purity:** destruction of Judah and House of David was a punishment for sins, Jews need to return to the pure worship of God so a Son of David can return to lead them (popular view with **Sadducees** and **Essenes**)

- **Military Action:** The Jews needed to rebel against the Romans so that the Son of David would appear to lead them to victory (popular with **Zealots** and some **Pharisees**)

Zealots: revolutionary sect founded by rogue Pharisees; opposed Roman occupation with violence, assassinations and civil war; hoped for Messiah to be a military leader; aimed to set up a new Davidic kingdom

1.1 ISAIAH'S SUFFERING SERVANT

Isaiah (8th century BCE): time of the destruction of the northern Kingdom of Israel; predicted defeat, slavery and humiliation for Kingdom of Judah too; also a prophecy of hope: a future Messianic Age when wars between empires will end and the Jews will be able to live in peace

> *The wolf will live with the lamb, the leopard will lie down with the goat, the calf and the lion and the yearling together; and a little child will lead them* – **Isaiah 11: 6**

'Suffering Servant': a figure described by Isaiah; serves God with total selflessness and loyalty; given a mission by God to lead the nations of the world; is mocked and attacked by the people God has sent him to help; endures his sufferings without complaining; is murdered; God returns the Servant to life and rewards him; people who had mistreated the Servant are ashamed.

> *He was despised and rejected by mankind, a man of suffering, and familiar with pain* – **Isaiah 53: 3**

Servant dies an ATONING DEATH = takes upon himself ***other people's*** pain and suffering, but nobody appreciates it.

> *But he was pierced for our transgressions, he was crushed for our iniquities; the punishment that brought us peace was on him, and by his wounds we are healed* – **Isaiah 53: 5**

Christian interpretation: predicts Jesus' atoning death and Resurrection which removes mankind's sins = FUTURIST

Jewish interpretation: the Servant is symbolic of 'Israel' (the entire Jewish nation, not the country) itself = PRETERIST

LINK TO KEY SCHOLAR: MORNA HOOKER

Jesus & the Servant (1959): OPPOSES the view the Suffering Servant predicts Jesus; line-by-line analysis of Isaiah and the Gospels shows no deliberate connection; argues that the Servant represents the Jewish nation collectively, not the future Messiah

> *Israel, who has been chosen by [God] as his servant, is to be restored from Exile and will manifest God's glory to all nations* – **Morna Hooker**

Link to: Topic 3.2 (Purpose of John) fulfilment of Scripture

1.1 THE MESSIANIC SECRET

Wilhem Wrede (1901): Jesus never claimed to be the Messiah; Jesus' original Disciples didn't believe he was the Messiah; 1st century Christians looked back on Jesus as the Messiah; this explains why Jesus keeps his Messiah-ship secret in **Mark's Gospel**:

> Jesus asks his disciples who they think he is: Peter answers, *"You are the Messiah"* and Jesus commands him to **keep this a secret**
>
> Jesus heals a leper: he orders the man **not to tell anyone** about this miracle

Jesus reveals that he is the Messiah in **Parables** so that his listeners cannot understand:

> *The secret of the kingdom of God has been given to you. But to those on the outside everything is said in parables* – **Mark 4: 11**

- **Markan Priority:** Mark is the first Gospel so this is the earliest record of Jesus' ministry

- **Historical Jesus:** Jesus' still-living friends/family knew he had never claimed to be the Messiah

- **Developing Christology:** 1st century Christians *did* claim he was the Messiah but argued that Jesus *kept it secret*

- **Redaction in the New Testament:** By the time of Matthew/Luke, Jesus' friends/family were dead so no need to present Messiah-ship as a secret

LINK TO KEY SCHOLAR: MORNA HOOKER

The Gospel According to St Mark (1993): it is plausible that Jesus would 'play down' his Messiah-ship (too politically explosive, distracted from his mission).

> if he believed himself to be in any sense the Messiah, the last thing he would do was to claim the title for himself - **Morna Hooker**

- **Matthean Priority:** many Catholics (in particular) continue to believe Matthew to be the first Gospel and it does not contain this 'secrecy' theme

- **Son of Man:** Jesus distances himself from the idea of the 'Messiah' and prefers the term **"Son of Man"**

> **Triumphal Entry:** Jesus arrives in Jerusalem and is greeted as a king (**Mark 11: 1-11** and ALL the other Gospels); makes no attempt to silence the crowd; arriving on a donkey which fulfils a prophecy from **Zechariah** about the Messiah: no secrecy here

Link to: Topic 3.1 **(Interpreting the Text)** Redaction Criticism

1.1 MATTHEW'S BIRTH NARRATIVE (Anthology #1)

 Morna Hooker says prologue works as a "*key*" to "*unlock*" each Gospel; Matthew's Prologue is the "*prophetic key*" because it focuses on Jesus as the Messiah and 'second Moses' predicted by the Old Testament prophets.

Joseph's dream: angel addresses Joseph as "*Joseph, Son of David*" - emphasizing the Joseph is of the line of David

Proof-Text #1: Isaiah predicted the Messiah would be born from a virgin

 The virgin will conceive and give birth to a son, and will call him Immanuel – **Isaiah 7: 14**

Futurist = predicts Jesus' virgin birth → ***"this took place to fulfil what the Lord had said through the prophet"***

Preterist = describes a royal birth back in the 8th century BCE (Prince Hezekiah of Judah)

LINK TO KEY SCHOLAR: RAYMOND E. BROWN

- **Translation error.** *almah* means "young woman" in Hebrew but Matthew translates this as "*parthenos*" in Greek, which means "virgin": did Matthew misunderstand Isaiah's prophecy?
- **Naturalistic explanation:** virgins conceive all the time: Isaiah was just hoping the mother of the young prince would conceive on her wedding night

Visit of the *Magi*: Gentile (non-Jewish) astrologers from Persia come to find Jesus; shows Jesus is "*a blessing to all the nations*" as god promised Abraham his descendant would be

Proof-Text #2: Prophet **Micah** predicts the Messiah would be born in Bethlehem; CRITERION OF EMBARRASSMENT (Jesus is famously from Nazareth in Galilee; this is embarrassing for 1st century Christians because it does not fit Micah's prophecy)

Proof-Text #3: Prophet **Hosea** writes about the Messiah coming back from Egypt; Matthew describes Jesus' family taking him to Egypt to escape King Herod then returning

Proof-Text #4: Prophet **Jeremiah** describes the Ruth weeping for her children; Matthew describes the mothers of Bethlehem weeping after King Herod murders all the babies there

 Raymond E. Brown says this echoes the story of **Moses**, where Pharaoh of Egypt gives orders to kill the male children of the Israelite slaves in **Exodus 1: 22**; Jesus is presented by Matthew as a "second Moses"; Brown believes this massacre is **symbolic**, not historical.

Contrast with: Topic 2.1 (Prologue in John) Word became Flesh

1.2 THE WORLD OF THE 1ˢᵗ CENTURY

Jesus lives in a region known as **Palestine** (modern Israel but including parts of Lebanon and Jordan with Egypt to the south and Syria to the north).

Inhabited by Jews descended from **Abraham** (perhaps 2000 BCE) and **Gentiles** (non-Jews, including Syrians, Phoenicians, Samaritans, Greeks and others).

Ruled by **King Herod the Great** (73-4 BCE), who was king when Jesus was born

Galilee: Northern territory around Lake Galilee; farming region of small villages and towns; mixture of Jews and Gentiles; Jesus grew up in **Nazareth**, a village in the hills of Galilee; ruled by **Herod Antipas**, son of King Herod the Great

- **Decapolis:** the 'Ten Cities', a region inhabited by Greek Gentiles and Hellenized Jews

- **River Jordan:** Flows from Sea of Galilee in the north down to the Dead Sea; forms the eastern border of Judea

Judea: Southern territory of mountains and deserts; mostly Jews, especially in the capital city of **Jerusalem**; Jesus is born in **Bethlehem**, a village 5 miles from Jerusalem

Jerusalem: ancient capital city of **King David** (about 1000 BCE) and holy city to 1ˢᵗ century Jews; contains the **Temple** where God is worshipped; every Spring thousands of Jewish pilgrims come here to celebrate **Passover**; Jesus is crucified here in 30 CE

- **Caesarea:** coastal fortress where the Roman governor rules – although the governor moves to Jerusalem every year to oversee the Passover celebrations

Samaria: Hilly region between Judea and Galilee; once the centre of the ancient Kingdom of Israel until it was destroyed in 722 BCE; inhabited by **Samaritans** who claim to be descended from ancient Israelites but Jewish leaders reject this; Jews were forbidden to have contact with Samaritans and often fought them

1.2 HELLENISM

International culture brought by Greeks and the Roman Empire; Greek ideas about politics, art, philosophy and religion; Greek language (*koine*) learned by all merchants and travelers.

Hellenization = the spread of Hellenic culture by force

Polytheism: the worship of many gods; the Twelve Gods of Olympus (headed by Zeus); very human (took human form, feuds and romances); full of psychological symbolism and meaning

- **Maccabee Revolt:** 168 BCE; King Antiochus imposed Hellenization; set up a statue of Zeus in the Jerusalem Temple; successful Jewish revolt by led the Maccabee brothers.

- Jews are monotheists; 1st Commandment forbids worshiping other gods

Art & Leisure: sculpture explored the human body in realistic detail and idealised it; theatre focused on human relationships and psychology (tragedies explored freewill, comedies poked fun at sex, religion and politics)

- **Gymnasium:** obsession with athletics and physical beauty; athletes competed naked

- **Bathing:** men and women (separately, not together) socialised naked

- Jews shocked by public nakedness; 2nd Commandment forbids making "*graven images*"

Rational Philosophy: ideas of Socrates Plato and Aristotle on science, ethics and metaphysics.

- **rational thought**, NOT religious revelation = contrast with the Jewish religion, which came from revelations given by God to Moses and the later prophets

LINK TO JESUS

Jesus grew up in Galilee (Hellenic ideas mixed with Jewish beliefs; e.g. theatre in Sepphoris near Nazareth); believed in life after death and personal immortality; gives his followers the 'Great Commission' in keeping with a Hellenic (universal) outlook rather than a purely-Jewish one.

 Therefore go and make disciples of all nations, baptizing them in the name of the Father and of the Son and of the Holy Spirit - **Matthew 28: 19**

John Dominic Crossan: Jesus was a Cynic philosopher; urged people to give up material possessions; Gadara; later followers viewed Jesus as the Suffering Messiah, which he had never claimed to be (= theory of the **Messianic Secret**)

Coming Kingdom of God: key teaching of Jesus; definitely not a Hellenic idea; more in the Prophetic tradition of the Old Testament

1.2 ROMAN OCCUPATION

Judea ruled directly by a Roman governor (**Pontius Pilate**); Galilee ruled by a 'client king' (**Herod Antipas**) backed by Roman military; rebellions always brewing because of heavy taxes and corrupt officials; Jewish beliefs and Messianic hopes produced more rebellion

Roman Emperors declared themselves to be the 'Son of God' (*Divi Filius*); Emperor Augustus placed his statues in temples to be worshiped; refusing to worship him was an act of rebellion as well as blasphemy.

Pontius Pilate: rank of 'prefect'; arrogant and insensitive to the Jewish religion; brought banners with pagan symbols into Jerusalem, triggering a riot; worked closely with the High Priest of the Temple in Jerusalem, **Joseph Caiaphas**

Judaism: considered *religio licita* - a protected religion; allowed to avoid sacrifices to pagan gods, working on the Sabbath; in return, Jewish priests in the Temple in Jerusalem sacrificed animals for the wellbeing of the Empire and the Emperor.

Publicans: local civil servants who collected taxes; able to demand bribes; these Jews were ostracized by their neighbours, sometimes threatened and killed; many abandoned Jewish faith

LINK TO JESUS

Jesus tells a **Parable of a Pharisee and a Publican** (Tax Collector): praises the humble faith of the publican and condemns the pride of the Pharisee; shocking for 1st century listeners

Mark 2: 15-17 describes Jesus being criticised for dining with publicans and replying that these sinners need God's love and forgiveness more than ordinary Jews; Jesus made converts of Zacchaeus, the chief publican of Jericho, and Matthew, a tax-collector in Capernaum (= author of Matthew's Gospel?)

Jesus asked whether a good Jew should pay taxes to Rome:

give back to Caesar what is Caesar's, and to God what is God's - **Matthew 22: 21**

Jesus was executed by Pontius Pilate; crucifixion a Roman punishment for rebels and runaway slaves; accused of opposing Roman Empire

A coin with the Emperor Tiberius' image – Jesus might have held just such a coin

"We have found this man subverting our nation. He opposes payment of taxes to Caesar and claims to be Messiah, a king." - **Luke 23: 2**

1.2 RELIGIOUS GROUPS IN PALESTINE

SADDUCEES: most influential Jewish sect; aristocratic and wealthy; based their religious beliefs entirely on the Torah (the first 5 books of the Old Testament); took the laws very literally; maintained the Temple in Jerusalem and sacrifices as detailed in the Old Testament.

- **Hellenic influences:** did not accept the Greek idea of the immortal soul, did not believe in life after death, rejected idea of a spirit world inhabited by angels, sceptical about miracles

- **Roman Occupation:** Sadducees worked with the Romans; **Caiaphas** was High Priest for 18 years and collaborated with **Pontius Pilate** to keep the peace

- **Jesus & the Sadducees:** opposite end of Jewish society from Jesus and his Galilean followers; Jesus argued with Sadducees about life after death; **Sanhedrin** (Sadducee council) condemned Jesus after he (allegedly) threatened to destroy the Temple.

 All four Gospels describe Jesus 'cleansing' the Temple by driving out the money-changers operating there; worshipers had to buy silver shekels to pay for sacrifices and this enriched the Sadducees; Jesus opposes their livelihood

PHARISEES: sect that opposed the Sadducees; much more popular among the ordinary people, especially in Galilee; followed the Oral Law (Torah + later prophets); a huge body of laws covering every area of Jewish life, from eating and washing to working, sex and death.

- **Hellenic influences:** believed in the immortal soul and in life after death, believed in a spirit world inhabited by angels; however also **anti-Hellenic**: Judaism provides a complete way of life superior to what was offered by the surrounding pagan culture

- **Roman Occupation:** Some Pharisees opposed Roman rule but most presented their religion as working alongside it

- **Jesus & the Pharisees:** Gospels show Jesus clashing with the Pharisees; accuses them of focusing too much on 'following the rules' and not enough on loving God; calls them **HYPOCRITES** (pretend to be good in public but in their private lives they are wicked)

 Jesus pronounces a series of "*woes*" (curses) on the Pharisees and others like them who treat religion as a set of rules to follow; calls them "*snakes*" and compares them to "*whitewashed tombs*" that look good on the outside but are rotten on the inside

PURITY: Jewish religion focuses on keeping spiritually pure; Sadducees did this through sacrifices in the Temple, Pharisees through obeying laws; purity could become more important than loving your neighbour and lead to spiritual pride (feeling that you are holier than anyone else); publicans and the sick were IMPURE or UNCLEAN; women were also considered unclean and excluded from worship and prayer

- Jesus rejected notions of purity and impurity: associated with publicans and women, ministered to the sick, freely broke rules like the Sabbath restrictions

TOPIC 1 EXAM QUESTIONS & REVISION ACTIVITIES

AS-Level Paper 3 (New Testament)

Section A

1   Explore key Old Testament prophecies regarding the birth of the Messiah. (9 marks)

2   Assess the significance of the Messianic secret for understanding the identity of Jesus. (9 marks)

3   Assess the significance of religious groups in Palestine at the time of Jesus. (9 marks)

Section B

4   (a) Explore the key ideas in Matthew's birth narrative. (8 marks)

(b) Analyse the view that Matthew's birth narrative provides the key to unlock the Gospel. (20 marks)

Total = 54 marks

A-Level Paper 3 (New Testament)

Section A

1   Explore key ideas regarding the Messianic Secret in Mark's Gospel. (8 marks)

2   Assess the significance of the political situation in 1st-century Palestine for the life and work of Jesus. (12 marks)

Section B

Read the following passage before answering the questions.

Joseph Accepts Jesus as His Son

[18] This is how the birth of Jesus the Messiah came about: His mother Mary was pledged to be married to Joseph, but before they came together, she was found to be pregnant through the Holy Spirit. [19] Because Joseph her husband was faithful to the law, and yet did not want to expose her to public disgrace, he had in mind to divorce her quietly.

[20] But after he had considered this, an angel of the Lord appeared to him in a dream and said, "Joseph son of David, do not be afraid to take Mary home as your wife, because what is conceived in her is from the Holy Spirit. [21] She will give birth to a son, and you are to give him the name Jesus, because he will save his people from their sins."

²² All this took place to fulfill what the Lord had said through the prophet: ²³ "The virgin will conceive and give birth to a son, and they will call him Immanuel" (which means "God with us").

²⁴ When Joseph woke up, he did what the angel of the Lord had commanded him and took Mary home as his wife. ²⁵ But he did not consummate their marriage until she gave birth to a son. And he gave him the name Jesus.

Quote from New International Translation, Matthew 1: 18-25

3 (a) Clarify the idea illustrated in this passage about Old Testament prophecies regarding the birth of the Messiah. *You must refer to the passage in your response.* (10 marks)

   (b) Assess the claim that Matthew's proof-texts are persuasive evidence for Jesus being the Messiah. (20 marks)

Section C

4 "The stories of Jesus' birth should not be taken as historically true."

   Evaluate this view in the context of prophecy regarding the Messiah. In your response to this question, you must include how developments in New Testament Studies have been influenced by one of the following:

   • Philosophy of Religion

   • Religion and Ethics

   • the study of a religion.

(30 marks)

Total = 90 marks

In these example papers, all the questions are drawn from Topic 1. A real exam would not be like this and each question would probably draw from a different Topic instead.

Comprehension Quiz

1   What is meant by prophecy?

2   What is the difference between a preterist and a futurist interpretation of prophecy?

3   What is a messiah?

4   Who was King David?

5   What is the Suffering Servant'?

6   Why does Wilhelm Wrede think Jesus keeps his Messiah-ship secret in Mark's Gospel?

7   What alternative explanation does Morna Hooker offer?

8   Explain what a proof-text is and give an example.

9   What is the significance of the Magi visiting Jesus' birth?

10 Who was King Herod?

11 What is the difference between Judea and Galilee?

12 What is a Gentile?

13 Give three examples of Hellenism.

14 Who was Pontius Pilate?

15 What's the difference between a Pharisee and a Sadducee?

Bible Quotes to match

Explain how each quote links to this Topic

1   *"The secret of the kingdom of God has been given to you. But to those on the outside everything is said in parables"* – **Mark 4: 11**

2   *The virgin will conceive and give birth to a son, and will call him Immanuel* – **Isaiah 7: 14**

3   *Your house and your kingdom will endure forever before me; your throne will be established forever* - **2 Samuel 7: 16**

4   *But he was pierced for our transgressions, he was crushed for our iniquities; the punishment that brought us peace was on him, and by his wounds we are healed* - **Isaiah 53: 5**

5   *"Therefore go and make disciples of all nations, baptizing them in the name of the Father and of the Son and of the Holy Spirit"* - **Matthew 28: 19**

6   *"We have found this man subverting our nation. He opposes payment of taxes to Caesar and claims to be Messiah, a king."* - **Luke 23: 2**

7   *The wolf will live with the lamb, the leopard will lie down with the goat, the calf and the lion and the yearling together; and a little child will lead them* - **Isaiah 11: 6**

Word Search

Find 20 terms/names from this Topic and explain them

```
T R V C F I B W G O X L W H E
N L G W T C J J R N X T U B G
V I E S M H P D B E R O M Y C
O C Q A W R O X M G D P C U V
F D G D R I N A E J H E Y Y H
J I V D J S T N E A H P H X E
R U C U P T I R R P J F A L A
N R D C H T U I O D Z U I J V
S K H E S S S R C O A T A Y S
S D W E A E P M L R N V S N P
H E L L E N I S M E Q Q I E E
X A E E L I L A G H D G W D P
P M E S S I A H F U R N D O D
V M S H R H T O H I G Z L O T
A E K I W T E G V G A X P F J
```

Crossword

Across

2. Interpreting prophecy to apply to the prophet's own time
3. A tax-collector for the Romans
7. Wicked king of the Jews
9. Greatest Old Testament prophet who received the Law from God
12. Old Testament prophet who wrote the Servant Songs
13. Gospel that describes Jesus' birth in Bethlehem
14. Region where Jesus grew up

Down

1. Greek culture
4. Greek translation of messiah
5. The anointed one
6. Jewish sect concerned with the Law
8. Greatest king of Israel
9. Old Testament prophet who predicted the Messiah would come from Bethlehem
10. Former Jewish kingdom, later a Roman province
11. Someone who isn't Jewish

Debates in this Topic

Indicate where you stand on this debate by marking a cross on th line then list points in favour and points against your position (more in favour the closer to the edge, more against the closer to the middle)

The New Testament persuades us that Jesus is the Messiah

The stories of Jesus' birth are not to be taken as historical

The 1st century context is essential to understand Jesus' identity and message

Jesus' ministry should be understood in a Jewish context

We cannot reconstruct the historical Jesus from the New Testament

Cloze Exercise

Jesus lived in 1st century_____, a region that covers the fertile hills around the Sea of _____and the mountains and deserts around the city of Jerusalem in_____. The Jewish people living here claimed descent from an ancestor called _____and worshiped one God by following a _____revealed to their greatest prophet Moses. The Old Testament consists of revelations to various Jewish prophets, many concerning the future arrival of a liberator called the Messiah, which means_____. 'Messiah' translated into Greek is_____.

1st century Jews had different expectations about what this messiah would be. Some expected a kingly messiah who would be a warlord who would drive out the occupying _____and set up a Jewish kingdom. Others expected a priestly messiah who would reform the corrupt _____in Jerusalem or a prophetic messiah who would bring in the end of the world.

Christians believe Jesus to be the promised messiah, despite him not fitting the expected description. Jesus did not lead a military campaign, set up a kingdom, reform the Jewish priesthood or bring about the end of the world. Also, he came from Galilee and did not seem to be descended from the royal line of_____.

_____'s Gospel corrects this impression in the story of Jesus' birth. The birth-narrative shows that Jesus was indeed descended from David through his father_____; Jesus was from_____, the home of the Messiah as predicted by the prophet_____; Jesus was born of a_____, as predicted by the Prophet Isaiah.

The Gospel makes other points about Jesus. It shows him to be the 'new Moses' when _____tries to kill all the babies in the region and Jesus' family escape to_____. It also shows _____ (non-Jews) recognizing Jesus' identity when the _____from the east visit his birthplace.

However, some scholars believe Jesus never claimed to be the Messiah. _____points out that in _____'s Gospel, Jesus keeps his messiah-ship a secret. This is explained by the fact that Jesus never really made such claims. Later Gospels, written after anyone who knew the historical Jesus had died, did not need to present this excuse of a _____ Secret.

Jesus' career brought him into conflict with other groups in Palestine. The legalistic _____objected to Jesus breaking rules like the Sabbath; the aristocratic _____felt threatened by Jesus' attack on their sacrifices in the Temple; the Roman governor _____eventually executed Jesus as a threat to Roman rule.

However, Jesus' followers interpreted what happened by comparing Jesus to the _____ in the Old Testament who dies for the sake of other people. They believed Jesus had died an _____death and was raised from the dead by God.

Abraham , 'anointed one', atoning, Bethlehem, Christ, Egypt, Galilee, Gentiles, Joseph, Judea, King David, King Herod, Law, Magi, Mark, Matthew, Messianic, Micah, Palestine, Pharisees, Pontius Pilate, Romans, Sadducees, Suffering Servant, Temple, virgin, Wrede

2 INTERPRETATION OF THE PERSON OF JESUS

2.1 THE PROLOGUE IN JOHN

This topic looks at the first 18 verses in John - the Johannine Prologue - and ideas about **the Word made flesh**, **light and dark**, **life**, **children of God**, **flesh and spirit**, **belief** and **law**, and **grace and truth**. The key scholars are **C.H. Dodd** and **Morna Hooker**.

2.3 MIRACLES & SIGNS

This topic looks at the 7 'Signs' (miracles) in John: **turning water into wine, healing the official's son, the healing at the pool, feeding the 5000, walking on water, healing the blind man** and **raising Lazarus**. The key scholars are **Raymond E. Brown** and **C.H. Dodd**.

2.2 TITLES OF JESUS & THE 'I AM' SAYINGS

This topic looks at the Jesus' titles in the Synoptic Gospels, including **Messiah**, **Son of God** and **Son of Man** as well as **Johannine "I Am" sayings** like **Bread of Life**, **Light of the World**, **Good Shepherd** and **True Vine**. The key scholars are **Raymond E. Brown** and **C.H. Dodd**.

KEY TERMINOLOGY:

Eucharist: Christian worship involving sharing bread and wine to commemorate Jesus' atoning death

Fourth Gospel: Another term for John's Gospel

Logos: Greek word for 'Word' or 'Thought'; philosophical idea of God's mind or plan as a force at work in the universe

Johannine: Related to John's Gospel

John the Baptist: Jewish preacher who was popular before Jesus' ministry; baptized people in the River Jordan to wash away their sins; executed by **Herod Antipas** around 31 CE.

Miracle: A violation of the laws of nature brought about by a supernatural force

Prologue: Introduction to a piece of writing that sets out its main ideas

Sabbath: Jewish day of rest on which work is forbidden

Sign: Word used in John's Gospel for 'miracle', suggesting hidden meanings

Son of Man: Term Jesus uses to describe himself; may refer to a cosmic judge or just an ordinary human being

2.1 THE PROLOGUE IN JOHN

John's Gospel: fourth and last Gospel in the New Testament; different from the previous three Synoptic Gospels; begins with 'prologue' which is a lengthy (18 verse) poem about Jesus that doesn't mention Jesus by name until the very end.

KEY SCHOLAR: MORNA HOOKER

Hooker says each Gospel's prologue works as a *"key"* to *"unlock"* the main themes:

The beginning of the story hints at the ideas that will be made plain at the end - **Mary Hooker**

"Glorious Key": Christ's supernatural character ('glory') as a divine being on Earth.

Was John's Prologue originally a hymn sung at church meetings and added to the Gospel later? → big change in style from the Prologue itself to the rest of the Gospel story; terms that are important in the Prologue (such as 'Logos') don't turn up again in the rest of the Gospel.

Morna Hooker disagrees: there is a prologue in all four Gospels, each with a 'break' or discontinuity where the prologue ends and the main Gospel begins.

"In the beginning": the **opening words of the Book of Genesis**; also the symbol of **Light**, which echoes God's **first creative act in Genesis: creating light**. Author is composing a new Genesis for a new religion

John the Baptist: These passages are interruptions and may come from a separate poem → two were merged together. Author does not refer to John as 'the Baptist' and does not refer to any baptisms: instead John is a *"witness"* to God's work and NOT the Logos/Light

"we have seen": rather than "I have seen"; scholars suggest the work of more than one person - a **JOHANNINE COMMUNITY** reporting their religious experiences

- There's no reference in the Prologue to the **Messiah** or the **line of David**
- There is no reference to the **Kingdom of God** arriving on Earth
- There's no **Birth Narrative** like in Matthew and Luke

KEY SCHOLAR: C.H. DODD

Is John's Gospel of late composition and Hellenic, not Jewish? uses **Hellenic terms** (like 'Logos' for the Word of God) – comes from the Greek world rather than the Jewish one that Jesus inhabited.

Dodd argues against this, pointing out the similarity between John's language and the Old Testament references to God's 'Word' and God's 'Holy Wisdom' *"dwelling"* among humans

2.1 KEY IDEAS IN JOHN'S PROLOGUE (Anthology #2)

WORD OF GOD BECOMING FLESH

Logos is a divine force that has existed since the beginning of the universe; it is part of God; events in the Old Testament where God speaks to prophets or performs miracles are actually the Logos; the Logos becomes a human being (INCARNATION) → this is person is Jesus Christ

Influence of Hellenism: 'Logos' is Greek; the philosopher **Heraclitus** first used it in 6th century BCE to describe the laws of nature; for 1st century philosophers, Logos is the World Soul that orders the according to logical principles (the word 'logical' comes from the word 'logos') --? An IMPERSONAL force

Scholars used to think that the Logos was en entirely Hellenic concept. However, **C.H. Dodd** challenges this view and shows that the Logos links to the way God is described in the Old Testament too.

Influences of Judaism: In **Book of Genesis**, God creates the world by SPEAKING; God calls to the prophets in speech; many Jews think of God's Word as separate from God himself; PERSONIFIED this Word of God as **Holy Wisdom**:

she is a reflection of eternal light, a spotless mirror of the working of God, and an image of his goodness - **Wisdom 7: 26**

Holy Wisdom *"makes her dwelling"* with the Jewish people and is symbolised by LIGHT

Morna Hooker distinguishes the idea that the human Jesus existed at the dawn of time from the idea that a divine quality that has always existed (**pre-existent**) became incarnated in Jesus.

'High' Christology: John's Gospel has a 'high' or INCARNATION view of Jesus as a divine power that has become human, vs the 'lower' EXALTATION Christology in the Synoptic Gospels where Jesus is seen as a human blessed with divine power

LIFE (or ETERNAL LIFE)

Life can be *zoë* (supernatural or spiritual life = immortal) or *bios* (physical life = must die) or *psyche* (mental life = can't exist without the body); humans have *bios/psyche* → get *zoë* through **believing in** Christ

For God so loved the world that he gave his one and only Son, that whoever believes in him shall not perish but have eternal life - **John 3: 16**

Debate over whether *zoë* life is experienced NOW or in the AFTERLIFE

C.H. Dodd distinguishes **quantitative** Life ("everlasting", no death, a typical belief of Pharisees) from **qualitative** Life (in the present moment, lived in a more fulfilled way, life of agape-love, no fear of death, this is a new view in John's Gospel)

LIGHT & DARKNESS

Light (Greek *phos*) is first thing to be created in **Genesis 1:3** when God's Word is spoken; God appears to the prophets in light and fire; Moses' face shines with God's reflected light; **symbol** for the Word of God: light gives rise to the physical (*bios*) life, through light we see the world and acquire mental (*psyche*) life → Light = the true knowledge of God.

Influence of Judaism: spiritual Light described in the Old Testament by **Isaiah**:

> *The people walking in darkness have seen a great light;*
> *on those living in the land of deep darkness, a light has dawned -* **Isaiah 9:2**

Darkness (Greek *skotos*) means **sin**; a type of blindness – unable or just refusing to see light of God; in John's Gospel many people who have physical (*bios*) sight and some who have intellectual (*psyche*) sight but they lack spiritual (*zoë*) sight: they are SPIRITUALLY BLIND

> *I am the light of the world. Whoever follows me will never walk in darkness, but will*
> *have the light of life –* **John 8: 12**

Prologue promises darkness never overcomes spiritual Light (reference to Jesus' Resurrection).

BELIEF (BELIEVING)

Believing is TRANSFORMATIVE: by believing, humans are transformed into **Children of God**.
Beliefs about (factual = ORTHODOXY) different from **believing** in (faith); Christians put their trust in Jesus, love and obey him, hope to be united with him

> *But these are written that you may believe that Jesus is the Messiah, the Son of God,*
> *and that by believing you may have life in his name -* **John 20: 31**

Evangelical Christians focus on transformational believing: "Born Again" movement, dramatic **conversion experience** → religion based on mere beliefs is sterile and dead if it doesn't lead to transformation into a **child of God**

CHILDREN OF GOD

Symbolic: trust God like a child trusts a father and be innocent and obedient; Synoptic Jesus says:

> *unless you change and become like little children, you will never enter the kingdom of*
> *heaven -* **Matthew 18: 3**

Spiritual re-birth: Christians who **believe in Jesus** are "*born of God*" vs "*natural descent*" (ancestors) - something chosen, a gift from God, not an accident; spiritual birth is **religious experience** → becoming a new person, making a fresh start.

C.H. Dodd argues Jews would consider themselves Children of God, because they are his Chosen People, descended from Abraham; **Morna Hooker** describes a *"gigantic take-over battle"*, with the Christians saying that they, not the Jews, are the true Chosen People (spiritual children, not biological children)

FLESH & SPIRIT

Flesh (Greek *sarx*) is the opposite of Spirit (Greek *pneuma*).

Flesh gives birth to flesh, but the Spirit gives birth to spirit – **John 3: 3**

Flesh means our physical (*bios*) Life vs spiritual (*zoë*) Life which is Spirit; *"according to the flesh"* includes everything that makes us human; **Word becomes Flesh** includes (1) racial identity (a Jew of **the line of David**), (2) political identity (a Galilean, living under **Roman occupation**), (3) family (the son of Mary and Joseph) and friends (Martha, Mary and Lazarus): → 'Born Again' of the Spirit means freedom from these identities

LAW

"The Law" (Greek, *ho nomos*) means Religious Law of the Jews: **'the Law of Moses'** or **'the Mosaic Law'**; commandments in first 5 books of the Old Testament (**TORAH**); e.g. dietary laws (eg the *kosher* rules for preparing food and banning pork) and Sabbath regulations; **Sadducees:** follow Written Torah; **Pharisees:** also include traditions outside the Torah, the Spoken Torah.

Christ is an ***alternative*** to the Law; **Moses** only sees God's back but Logos (Jesus) sees God face-to-face: much closer relationship than Moses ever had → selfless love (*agape*) is the ***real*** way of following the Law:

Whoever loves others has fulfilled the Law – **Romans 13: 8**

ANTINOMIANISM is a complete rejection of the Law; **Gnostic** heretics in the 2nd century vs orthodox Christians who still obeyed the Ten Commandments; ongoing debate about which Old Testament laws still apply to Christians (e.g. diet, blood transfusions, Sabbath, homosexuality)

GRACE & TRUTH

Grace (Greek, *charis*) links to Glory (*doxa*): "*Charis*" means "favour" or "gift" (connected to 'charity') whereas "*doxa*" refers to God's awesome reality, a **numinous religious experience**.

Prologue claims *"we have seen God's Glory"* = God appearing through Jesus → old Grace (**Law of Moses**) v; new Grace given to ***everyone*** (including Gentiles) *"in place of"* the Law

Truth (Greek, *aletheia*) because Jesus brings the Truth about God - the genuine **revelation** about what God is like; superior to the Jewish Law.

Influences of Hellenism: Greek philosopher **Plato** tells story about prisoners in a cave who mistake the shadows for reality until one prisoner escapes and learns the Truth about reality; other prisoners in the cave do not believe him → Jesus comes from the God and tries to tell humanity the Truth but Jesus' own people, the Jews, do not believe him.

You will know the truth, and the truth will set you free - **John 8: 32**

2.2 TITLES OF JESUS IN THE SYNOPTIC GOSPELS

'Synoptic' = "*seen together*": **Matthew**, **Mark** and **Luke** share passages that are word-for-word the same and other passages where one Gospel has taken text from the other and either added or taken parts out

- **Matthew** focuses on Jesus as the **prophesied Jewish Messiah**

- **Mark** focuses on Jesus as the **Suffering Servant** who moves **in secret** among his people

- **Luke** presents Jesus as the **Saviour** of all people, including Gentiles (non-Jews)

- Synoptics are **descriptive** rather than reflective: miracles and healings; encounters with the Jewish and Roman authorities, with lunatics and with ordinary people; casting out demons.

TITLE: MESSIAH

Hebrew **Mashiach** = "**the anointed one**," or "**the chosen one**": prophets, priests, and kings were anointed by pouring oil into the hair and beard to make it shine; → a **particular** person who was chosen by God, a FUTURE SAVIOUR or LIBERATOR; **Christos** (Christ) is Greek for Messiah:

 Jesus asks his Disciples who people think that he is (**Mark 8:27-30**). Answers: the prophet Elijah come back to Earth, John the Baptist restored to life. Jesus asks them who **they** think he is. Peter answers: "*You are the* Christos" (=*Messiah*)

- A descendent of King David (**Isaiah 11: 1**)

- Born in Bethlehem in Judea (**Micah 5: 2**)

- **Kingly Messiah** will drive out the occupying Romans and rule an independent Jewish kingdom

- **Priestly Messiah** will reform the corrupt Temple in Jerusalem and abolish **Sadducees**

- **Prophetic Messiah** will arrive before Judgement Day

- **Suffering Messiah** will die an atoning death for the sake of mankind = Christian view

Proof-texts (quotes from the Old Testament) show Jesus is the Messiah; Jesus' life doesn't fit the expectations about the Messiah: a Galilean from Nazareth, not a Judean from Bethlehem (CRITERON OF EMBARRASSMENT: Christians would not invent such embarrassing details so probably historical): **Matthew** = Jesus born in Bethlehem but left because of King Herod; **Luke** = Jesus' family was visiting Bethlehem for a census but then returned home to Galilee

Messianic Secret (tendency for **Mark's Gospel** to show Jesus being secretive about his Messiah-ship); William Wrede (1901) argues Jesus never claimed to be the Messiah: later Christians invented this but presented it as a 'secret' so long as Jesus' friends/relatives still alive

TITLE: SON OF GOD

Hellenic Influences: First Roman Emperor, **Augustus**, used the initials **D.F.**, which stand for *divi filius* ('son of the divine one') or *dei filius* ('son of God'); also used by the next Emperor, **Tiberius**, during Jesus' lifetime.

One of Augustus' coins, declaring him to be the son of God

Jewish influences: belief in one God who is a spirit and does not come to Earth to mate with human women; **blasphemy** for Jews.

 C.H. Dodd argues that 1st century Jews expected the Messiah to be the 'son of God': but **symbolic** to mean someone specially chosen by God, sent by God and blessed by God - NOT a **literal** child born to God.

Christian view = **Jesus is a human in whom God is uniquely present**.

- Jesus **reveals God** in everything he says and does: forgives sins, calls God *'Father'*.

- Jesus perfectly **surrenders his will** to God — **perfect human** with perfect relationship with God

Mark's Gospel begins by calling Jesus the "Son of God" but Jesus himself never calls himself 'Son of God' directly; **Matthew** describes the Disciples calling Jesus "Son of God"; **Matthew** and **Luke** birth-narratives include angels revealing that Jesus is the 'Son of God' → Did the idea of Jesus being the 'Son of God' develop LATER among 1st century Christians?

 The sayings and deeds of Jesus reported in the Gospels have been influenced by hindsight after the Resurrection - **Raymond E. Brown**

TITLE: SON OF MAN

Aramaic title (*bar-nash*) = language Jesus and his Disciples actually spoke; one of Jesus' favourite terms for himself; scholars call this IPSISSIMA VERBA = the ***actual words*** of Jesus

 the Son of Man did not come to be served, but to serve, and to give his life as a ransom for many - **Matthew 20: 8**

Refers to Jesus' humanity vs than **Son of God** (= Jesus' divinity)

- **Coming Son of Man** who will rule on Judgment Day (prophecy by **Daniel** in Old Testament)

- **Suffering Son of Man** who will be tortured and killed (**Suffering Servant** of **Isaiah**)

- **Faithful Son of Man** who is God's humble servant (God refers to **Ezekiel** this way in Old Testament)

 The Son of Man has authority on earth to forgive sins - **Mark 2: 10**

2.1 "I AM" STATEMENTS IN JOHN (Anthology #3)

God identified himself to Moses by the name "I AM" = YHWH or YAHWEH in Hebrew → Jesus identifies himself as God y speaking this way

> *"I am who I am. This is what you are to say to the Israelites: "I am has sent me to you" - Exodus 3: 14*

These are the 7 "I AM" statements in John's Gospel (capitalized one are in Anthology):

1. I AM THE BREAD OF LIFE
2. I AM THE LIGHT OF THE WORLD
3. I am the gate for the sheep
4. I AM THE GOOD SHEPHERD
5. I am the resurrection and the life
6. I am the way, the truth, and the life
7. I AM THE TRUE VINE

I AM THE BREAD OF LIFE

Midrash: a Jewish term for interpretation of a Biblical passage; Jesus provides a Sign but crowds take it at literal level, so Jesus explains deeper meaning in a *midrash*

> Jesus miraculously **feeds the 5000**; Jesus is offering **spiritual bread** that provides spiritual life vs **Moses**, who provided miraculous food to eat called *manna* which only fed the body

The real bread he is offering to his followers is HIMSELF; followers need to **believe in him** to receive this Bread of Life → eat his body and drink his blood → the **EUCHARIST** (bread = body of Christ, wine = blood of Christ) which commemorates Christ's atoning death → share in his Resurrection

> **Raymond E. Brown** does not think Jesus really said these words: they would have made no sense to 1st century Jews before the Eucharistic ceremony had been invented → this SACRAMENTAL theme was added in later by Christians

Implications: John's Gospel does not contain **Last Supper** (in all three Synoptic Gospels, Jesus shares a Passover meal with his Disciples, instructs them to eat bread and drink wine in memory of him) → this *midrash* introduces the Eucharist instead (and the **Feeding of the 5000** is at Passover too).

Eucharist debate: Roman Catholics = bread and wine really becomes Christ's body and blood (TRANSUBSTANTIATION) vs **Protestants** = bread and wine are purely **symbolic**; debate about 'Real Presence' of Christ in Eucharist → warfare between different Christians in the past.

Link to: Sign of Feeding the 5000

I AM THE LIGHT OF THE WORLD

Link to **Light and Darkness** in Prologue; **Isaiah 49: 6** prophesied that Messiah would be a "*light to the Gentiles*" and **Isaiah 42: 7** said he would "*open eyes that are blind*": passage concerns **a man who was born blind;** links to in 1st century Judaism's belief that illness = punishment for sin; Jesus rejects this view → real problem is SPIRITUAL BLINDNESS and Jesus is the cure

> **Raymond E Brown** views blindness **symbolizing** ignorance of Judaism; the '*works of god will be displayed*' in them when they convert to Christianity → fulfills prophecy about the Messiah *opening eyes* and *being a light*
>
> *The blind man knows little and yet learns much; the Pharisees know everything and can be taught nothing* - **Raymond E. Brown**

Implications: use of candles in Christian worship; PASCHAL CANDLE lit on Easter Sunday → symbolizes **Light** & hope of **Eternal Life**; **Augustine of Hippo** views being "*born blind*" as reference to **original sin:** *"the blind man is the human race"*

Link to: Sign of Healing the Blind Man

I AM THE GOOD SHEPHERD

Sheep = Jewish people ("*lost sheep of Israel*" **Matthew 15: 24**), Jesus = gate to **Eternal Life**

> **Raymond E. Brown** says "*thieves and robbers*" = **Pharisees**: they *claim* to offer the way to God through **legalism** (following laws); they don't represent sort of religion God wants; ordinary people can't keep all the rules (sheep "*have not listened to them*") → they can **believe in Jesus**

'Hirelings' only guard because they are (poorly) paid vs **Good Shepherd** motivated by love.

> When Jesus talks about '*laying down his life for his sheep*' = Crucifixion; King David fought lions and survived; Jesus will confront the **Sadducees and the Pharisees** and the **Roman Empire**, but dies atoning death to save people from sin.

Implications: Christian leaders = **pastors** (Latin for 'shepherd'); bishops carry a **crozier,** (shepherd's crook); hierarchical orthodox church vs egalitarian John's Gospel arguing Christ is the true 'pastor' of the church so no need for leaders and ranks

I AM THE TRUE VINE

Jesus = vine in a vineyard; **God** = gardener; **cutting away branches** = people who don't truly believe going to Hell/leaving when persecuted; healthy branches producing fruit = true believers

Vine = Jewish nation ('Israel') → Christianity is the true 'Israel' and God's promises apply to them, not Jews; useless branches = **Pharisees** whose religion is also about appearances, not love

Implications: "*fruits of the Holy Spirit*" is developed by **Paul** and the greatest fruit is Love; idea that *agape*-love is at the heart of Christian ethics → **Situation Ethics**

2.3 MIRACLES & SIGNS

Synoptic Gospels use Greek word *'dynamis'* (act of power) for miracle; includes healing people with disabilities, driving out demons and *'unclean spirits'* (EXORCISMS), multiplying food and walking on water → **David Hume**: *"a transgression of a law of nature"*

- **Hypnotism:** healings caused by PLACEBO EFFECT (caused by belief in the cure); lunatics healed by being shown compassion → not possible to hypnotise crowds of non-consenting people, some sufferers have clear physical disabilities

- **Illusions/theatrics:** tricks of stage magic (e.g. **walking on water** was really walking on a sandbank); disabled people were faking illness; charlatanism (trying to hoax people) vs spiritual theatre (using staged 'miracles' to make spiritual points) → but Jesus prepared to be executed for beliefs; in **Mark** Jesus keeps his miracles secret

John's calls miracles *semeion* ('**Signs**'): only 7 Signs., no exorcisms, even more outrageously impossible than the miracles in the Synoptic Gospels → difficult to explain as hypnotism but very symbolic so may be **spiritual theatre**

> **Raymond E. Brown** argues John's Gospel *deliberately* makes it hard to take Signs literally: Jesus creates the best wine anyone has drunk; raises a dead man's rotting corpse → spiritual meaning is more important than literal events

1st SIGN: TURNING WATER INTO WINE (links to: I am the True Vine)

- Jesus, his Disciples and mother (**Mary**, but unnamed in **John**) attend a wedding at **Cana** (near Nazareth) and the wine runs out
- Mary asks Jesus to help; he refuses but then tells servants to fill jars with water and serve it
- Water becomes wine and master of ceremony (best man) is amazed at the quality

3rd day: link to 3rd day in Genesis (creation of plants, vines, fruit) and 3rd day in Gospels (Resurrection)

"Woman": links Mary to Eve, mother of a new Creation

Jars: used for Jewish purification but empty = emptiness of Jewish rituals

Wine: Christianity replacing Judaism; intoxication replacing sterility; joy replacing duty

"saved the best wine till last": Jesus is superior to the Old Testament prophets

Identity of Jesus: Jesus is the true bridegroom (church is the bride), Jesus is the source of joy (on his Resurrection), Jesus is intoxicating believers (with his Holy Spirit)

Implications: establishes the **EUCHARIST** (Communion wine - Cana symbolises the Eucharist and the guests are the congregation); God's approval of marriage, sex and pleasure → debate over CELIBACY and ASCETICISM (giving up sex and pleasure) in the church.

2nd SIGN: HEALING THE OFFICIAL'S SON (links to: I am the Way, the Truth and the Life)

- Returning to Galilee, Jesus stops in **Cana** and is met by an official of Herod Antipas whose son is dying
- Official asks Jesus for help, Jesus criticizes him for being a miracle-seeker not a believer
- Official perseveres, Jesus promises him his son will live
- On journey home to Capernaum, Official hears his son has recovered

3rd day: link to 3rd day in Gospels (Resurrection)

"took Jesus at his word": represents believing in Jesus as the Word of God

"whole household believed": a community transformed by believing in Jesus

"Your son will live": Son restored to *bios*-life but Jesus also offers *zoë*-life to those who believe in him; Jesus is also the 'son' (of God) who will live even though he dies

Identity of Jesus: Jesus is the source of Life (*bios* and *zoë*); Jesus answers prayers; believers must *take Jesus at his word* and have faith that he will save them

Implications: Christians make PETITIONARY PRAERS (asking for daily bread, delivering from temptation, healing, help); Jesus teaches the 'Lord's Prayer'; this Sign is a model for how prayer should be (not testing God or looking for miracles but sincere and confident in God's love)

3rd SIGN: HEALING AT THE POOL (links to: I am the Door)

- Jesus visits Jerusalem; at Sheep's Gate Pool (Bethesda) there is superstition the waters can heal sickness
- Invalid has been sick for 38 years because he cannot get to the waters on time
- Jesus tells him to pick up his mat and walk away
- It is the Sabbath so the Jewish leaders are angry that the rules have been broken

The Pool: an *asclepion* (sacred pool dedicated to pagan god of healing), represents superstition (paganism, also Pharisees)

"38 years": reference to 39 *melachot* (types of work forbidden on the Sabbath)

"whole household believed": a community transformed by believing in Jesus

"Pick up your mat": Carrying a burden is the 39th *melacha* (forbidden type of work)

"The man who made me well": he does not know who Jesus is (neither do the Jewish leaders)

Identity of Jesus: Jesus is the source of healing, not pagan superstition; Jesus is the 'Lord of the Sabbath' and can break Sabbath rules because he is the source of the Torah

Implications: Jesus is the truth behind pagan myths and superstitions; those who are sick and recover do not realise that Jesus is responsible for al healing and health; Sabbath regulations do not apply to Christians; trying to please God by following laws is a paralyzing sickness;

4th SIGN: FEEDING OF THE 5000 (links to: I am the Bread of Life)

- Back in Galilee, Jesus gathers a huge crowd but there is no food for them
- A boy has 5 loaves and 2 fish and Jesus orders these to be shared
- Everyone is seated and eats
- There are 12 baskets of food left over
- The crowd wants to crown Jesus 'King of the Jews' but he escapes

3rd day: link to 3rd day in Gospels (Resurrection)

"small loaves of bread": probably flat unleavened bread = a Passover meal

5 loaves: might symbolise 5 wounds on the cross (hands, feet, side)

fish: a Christian symbol (ICHTHYS)

12 baskets: 12 symbolises perfection: the 12 tribes of Israel, feeding the Jewish nation spiritually

Identity of Jesus: Jesus is the **bread of life**; he is the source of spiritual life just a bread nourishes the body; Jesus is also the source of fertility – *"Be fruitful and increase in number"* (**Genesis 1: 22**)

Implications: Another Sign that establishes the EUCHARIST (bread here, wine at Cana); Disciples hand out the food, representing the authority Jesus passes on to the church; debate about whether the miracle is multiplication (supernatural) or sharing (naturalistic)

5th SIGN: WALKING ON WATER (links to: I am the Good Shepherd)

- Following on from the last Sign, the Disciples take a boat across the Sea of Galilee without Jesus
- Night falls, a storm blows in, they are afraid
- Jesus walks across the water to them
- He enters the boat, the storm ceases, they have arrived at the other shore

"By now it was dark": darkness symbolizes sin and ignorance; Jesus' followers try to act without his Light and fail

"The waters grew rough": symbolises persecution and hardship faced by believers

"They were frightened": a **numinous** religious experience

"they were willing to take him in": symbolizes willingness to believe in Christ, to be born again

Identity of Jesus: Jesus is Lord of the natural world who controls the elements; he is the Light that guides people in the darkness and they are lost without him; he protects his Church even when it seems he is far away

Implications: Easy to interpret as a hallucination (exhaustion) or illusion (sandbank, according to **Schweitzer**) except for 'teleporting' at the end; reference to Christians enduring persecution (e.g. hiding in the catacombs of Rome)

6th SIGN: HEALING THE BLIND MAN (links to: I am the Light of the World)

- In Jerusalem, Jesus meets a man born blind; he makes paste out of dust and spittle, smears it on the man's eyes and tells him to wash it off in the Pool of Siloam
- The **Pharisees** are angry because the Sabbath regulations have been broken
- Being interrogated by the Pharisees strengthens the man's faith

"mud with the saliva": making clay is a *melacha* (forbidden work on the Sabbath); it echoes God making Adam out of earth in **Genesis 2: 7** (Jesus is making this person a new man)

Pool of Siloam: = 'Sent'; indicates Jesus is sending man on a spiritual journey (blindness may be symbolic for spiritual blindness)

"I am the man": the man has been changed, his neighbours do not recognise him (symbolizes change from a conversion experience); also 'the man' is how Adam is referred to in **Genesis**

"We are disciples of Moses": Pharisees believe in their traditions, not the miracles in front of them; they are the real blind men

Identity of Jesus: Jesus is the Light but his enemies prefer to live in Darkness; Jesus repeats God's creative work in **Genesis**; Jesus can ignore the Sabbath because his Father does

Implications: Christian antisemitism: Jews are willfully blind, people of darkness, they persecute those who see the light, their authority comes from fear not love; later Christians called Jews "*assassins of Christ*"

7th SIGN: RAISING LAZARUS FROM THE DEAD (links: "I am the Resurrection & the Life")

- In **Bethany**, Lazarus is dying; Jesus travels from the River Jordan but delays so that **Lazarus** dies before he arrives
- Lazarus' sisters **Mary** & **Martha** have faith in Jesus; Jesus visits the tomb and weeps
- They open the tomb; Jesus calls Lazarus to come out
- Lazarus rises, still wrapped in grave clothes which Jesus orders to be removed
- The Jewish priests, led by **Caiaphas**, decide to have Jesus killed

"resurrection at the last day": Pharisee belief that the dead will be raised on Judgment Day; Jesus offers a different sort of Eternal Life from this

4 days: = Lazarus is 4 days dead; contrast with Jesus who rises from death on the 3rd day; similarly, Jesus rolls his own stone away and leaves his grave clothes behind

"let him go": grave clothes represent the Jewish Law; Law belongs to death not life and believers are free when they follow Christ not the Law

"one man die for the people": Without realizing, the High Priest describes Jesus' atoning death

Identity of Jesus: Jesus is the source of *zoë*-Life (Eternal Life); this Sign describes Jesus' Resurrection but Lazarus cannot do what Jesus does unassisted and only rises back to *bios*-life

Implications: Lazarus represents the early Christians: persecuted, abandoned, dead as far as their Jewish families were concerned, brought together as a community by Christ's love, freed from the Jewish Law (further evidence of Christian antisemitism too)

TOPIC 2 EXAM QUESTIONS & REVISION ACTIVITIES

AS-Level Paper 3 (New Testament)

Section A

1   Explore the key ideas in the Prologue of John's Gospel. (9 marks)

2   Assess the significance of the 'I am' sayings in the Fourth Gospel. (9 marks)

3   Assess the strengths of the view that 'Son of God' is the most important of Jesus' titles in the Synoptic Gospels (9 marks)

Section B

4   (a) Explore the key ideas of two Signs in the Fourth Gospel. (8 marks)

(b) Analyse the view that the Signs are vital for understanding Jesus' ministry. (20 marks)

Total = 54 marks

A-Level Paper 3 (New Testament)

Section A

1   Explore the key ideas in the Prologue of John's Gospel. (8 marks)

2   Assess the view that the 'I am' sayings in the Fourth Gospel reveal the identity of Jesus. (12 marks)

Section B

Read the following passage before answering the questions.

[5] When Jesus looked up and saw a great crowd coming toward him, he said to Philip, "Where shall we buy bread for these people to eat?" [6] He asked this only to test him, for he already had in mind what he was going to do.

[7] Philip answered him, "It would take more than half a year's wages to buy enough bread for each one to have a bite!"

[8] Another of his disciples, Andrew, Simon Peter's brother, spoke up,[9] "Here is a boy with five small barley loaves and two small fish, but how far will they go among so many?"

[10] Jesus said, "Have the people sit down." There was plenty of grass in that place, and they sat down (about five thousand men were there). [11] Jesus then took the loaves, gave thanks, and distributed to those who were seated as much as they wanted. He did the same with the fish.

¹² When they had all had enough to eat, he said to his disciples, "Gather the pieces that are left over. Let nothing be wasted." ¹³ So they gathered them and filled twelve baskets with the pieces of the five barley loaves left over by those who had eaten.

Quote from New International Translation, John 6: 5-13

3   (a) Clarify the ideas illustrated in this passage about the identity and role of Jesus as expressed in this passage. *You must refer to the passage in your response.* **(10 marks)**

(b) Assess the claim that Signs are important for understanding Jesus' ministry. **(20 marks)**

Section C

4   "Jesus' ministry shows he is the Son of God."

Evaluate this view in the context of the interpretation of the person of Jesus. In your response to this question, you must include how developments in New Testament Studies have been influenced by one of the following:

- Philosophy of Religion

- Religion and Ethics

- the study of a religion.

(30 marks)

Total = 90 marks

In these example papers, all the questions are drawn from Topic 2. A real exam would not be like this and each question would probably draw from a different Topic instead..

Comprehension Quiz

1   What is meant by a prologue?

2   What is the Logos?

3   How is John's Gospel different from the Synoptic Gospels?

4   What is meant by believing in Jesus?

5   How does John's Gospel refer back to the Old Testament?

6   What do Christians mean by 'Son of God'?

7   Why does Jesus call himself the 'Son of Man'?

8   What is significant about the phrase "I am"?

9   Identify three "I am" statements made by Jesus in John's Gospel.

10   What is the Eucharist?

11   What is the Sabbath?

12   Which two Signs did Jesus perform at Cana?

13   Which two Signs did Jesus perform in Jerusalem?

14   How much food was involved in the feeding of the 5000?

15   What does the symbolism mean in the raising of Lazarus from the dead?

Bible Quotes to match

Explain how each quote links to this Topic

1   *"the Son of Man did not come to be served, but to serve, and to give his life as a ransom for many"* - **Matthew 20: 8**

2   *"I am who I am. This is what you are to say to the Israelites: "**I am** has sent me to you"* - **Exodus 3: 14**

3   *Whoever loves others has fulfilled the Law* – **Romans 13: 8**

4   *For God so loved the world that he gave his one and only Son, that whoever believes in him shall not perish but have eternal life* - **John 3: 16**

5   *"I am the light of the world. Whoever follows me will never walk in darkness, but will have the light of life"* – **John 8: 12**

6   *But these are written that you may believe that Jesus is the Messiah, the Son of God, and that by believing you may have life in his name* - **John 20: 31**

7   *"Be fruitful and increase in number"* – **Genesis 1: 22**

Word Search

Find 20 terms/names from this Topic and explain them

```
S  J  W  Z  W  V  N  L  S  C  Z  R  M  S  H
O  O  L  A  G  I  E  S  E  Y  W  L  F  W  K
N  Z  N  O  T  N  C  P  I  A  N  I  H  M  U
O  W  M  O  F  E  A  I  U  J  P  G  G  S  Q
F  C  G  N  F  U  R  R  G  K  Z  H  N  W  A
M  C  Q  I  G  G  G  I  V  X  X  T  S  W  W
A  G  L  H  L  O  O  T  N  F  G  U  A  P  B
N  A  K  W  F  L  W  D  V  T  R  R  H  T  M
N  S  A  K  X  O  A  I  K  A  O  T  P  L  H
A  X  L  W  F  R  E  A  Z  J  A  W  A  G  K
P  K  B  O  K  P  F  A  F  B  R  N  I  P  Z
R  S  R  N  G  I  L  L  B  E  T  H  A  N  Y
P  I  E  R  D  O  E  A  R  X  U  O  C  C  E
G  S  A  B  C  R  S  E  R  F  N  F  B  P  Z
S  N  D  L  X  X  H  I  P  E  K  A  U  T  N
```

Crossword

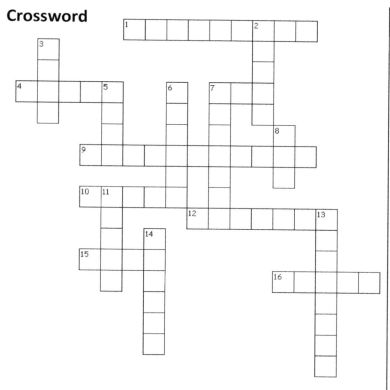

Across
1. Pharisee who visited Jesus
4. The Word of God
7. Son of ___, cosmic judge in the Book of Daniel
9. When a spirit takes on physical form
10. Opposite of the Spirit
12. Jesus raised him from the dead
15. Four letters representing God's name in Hebrew
16. The supernatural quality of God and Christ

Down
2. Bread from Heaven that fed the Israelites in the desert
3. Greek word for physical life
5. Name for a miracle in John's Gospel
6. _____ Gospel, alternative name for John's Gospel
7. Type of work forbidden on the Sabbath
8. Greek word for eternal life
11. First thing created by God
13. Greek for 'seen together'
14. Greek for 'messiah'

Debates in this Topic

Indicate where you stand on this debate by marking a cross on the line then list points in favour and points against your position (more in favour the closer to the edge, more against the closer to the middle)

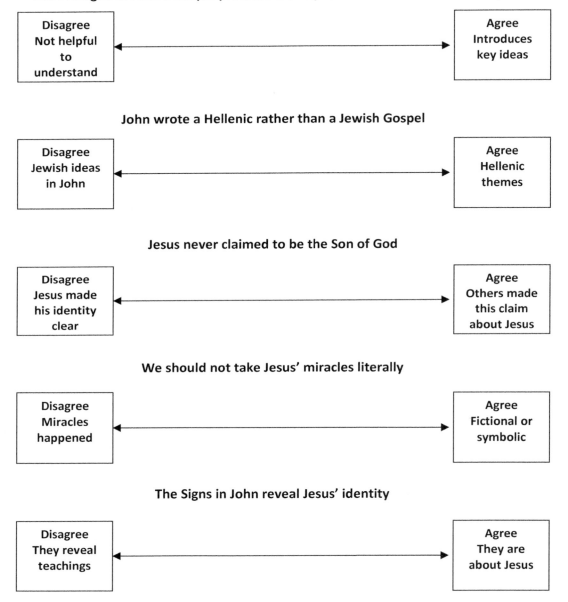

The Prologue of John's Gospel provides the key to unlock the rest of the Gospel

| Disagree Not helpful to understand | | Agree Introduces key ideas |

John wrote a Hellenic rather than a Jewish Gospel

| Disagree Jewish ideas in John | | Agree Hellenic themes |

Jesus never claimed to be the Son of God

| Disagree Jesus made his identity clear | | Agree Others made this claim about Jesus |

We should not take Jesus' miracles literally

| Disagree Miracles happened | | Agree Fictional or symbolic |

The Signs in John reveal Jesus' identity

| Disagree They reveal teachings | | Agree They are about Jesus |

Cloze Exercise

Of the four Gospels, Matthew, Mark and _____are 'Synoptic' which means '_____' because they share so much material and exact wording. John's Gospel, sometimes called the _____Gospel, is different, sharing only _____ of its vocabulary with the others.

The Synoptic Gospels present Jesus as the _____promised in the Old Testament. However, they present him as an unusual version who suffers and dies an atoning death rather than as a king or reforming priest. They also present Jesus as the Son of God. In the Old Testament, this means someone especially blessed by God but in the pagan world it means someone literally descended from a god or possessing a god's powers. Christians disagreed about how to interpret this, with some following a _____ Christology where Jesus is _____by God when he is baptised or _____by God when he is raised from the dead; others followed a _____Christology where Jesus is God _____in human form.

Jesus describes himself as the_____, an expression which describes a cosmic judge in the prophecy of _____but also suggests an ordinary human being who serves God faithfully.

John's Gospel begins with a _____which introduces Jesus as the Word of God by using the Greek word _____to describe him. This is an immortal spirit from the dawn of time who is part of God and delivered God's revelations to the _____in the Old Testament but is now living as a human being. A big theme in John's Gospel is the importance of _____in Jesus as the Word of God and being spiritually transformed by this belief; Jesus calls this being '_____'.

John's Gospel shows that Jesus is part of God when he uses the phrase "_____" to identify himself: this phrase in _____is the holy name of God revealed to _____in the Old Testament.

John's Gospel also uses Signs to show who Jesus is and illustrate his teachings. Unlike the _____in the Synoptic Gospels, these Signs are very_____. For example, the Sign of Healing the _____represents Jesus providing spiritual enlightenment to people who are blind to the truth about God; it links to Jesus' claim to be the_____.

Brown argues that several Signs have a sacramental meaning to them, which explains the importance of the _____where Christians worship by eating bread and drinking wine. They also have a _____meaning, encouraging Christians to have faith, give generously and not to worry about Jewish laws like the _____regulations.

The greatest Sign is when Jesus raises _____from the dead. This foreshadows Jesus' own death and resurrection, since the dead man is raised from a _____just like the one Jesus will be put in. However, the Risen Jesus leaves behind his _____since he has overcome death, whereas the dead man still wears his since he will need them again.

10%, adopted, believing, Blind Man, Born Again, Daniel, Eucharist, exalted, Fourth, grave clothes, Hebrew, high, I Am, incarnated, Lazarus, Light of the World, Logos, low, Luke, Messiah, miracles, Moses, Prologue, prophets, Sabbath, sapiential, seen together, Son of Man, symbolic, tomb

3 INTERPRETING THE TEXT

3.1 INTERPRETING THE TEXT

This topic looks at the **Synoptic Problem** (including **proto-Gospels**, the **priority of Mark**, *Q* **source**, **2-source** and **4-source solutions**) as well as **source criticism, form criticism** and **redaction criticism**

3.2 THE PURPOSE & AUTHORSHIP OF THE FOURTH GOSPEL

This topic looks at different theories about John's Gospel, including **purpose** (including **spiritual Gospel, life in his Name, Christ, Son of God, fulfilling Scripture** and **conversion**) and **authorship**. The key scholars are **Raymond E. Brown** and **C.H. Dodd**.

KEY TERMINOLOGY:

Beloved Disciple: Mysterious figure who appears from chapter 13 of **John's Gospel**; may represent the author of John's Gospel

Form Criticism: Interpretation of the Bible based on its origins as *pericopae* circulating among the first Christian communities

Fourth Gospel: Another name for **John's Gospel**

Johannine Community: Community of Jewish Christians expelled from the Synagogues, perhaps in Antioch c. 90 CE; composed **John's Gospel**; perhaps led by the **Beloved Disciple**

Markan Priority: Theory that **Mark** is the earliest Gospel and was copied by **Matthew** and **Luke**

Pericope: In **Form Criticism**, a textual unit that was original a memory of Jesus passed on by word of mouth before the Gospels were written (plural *pericopae*)

Proto-Gospel: Theoretical early Gospel which is now lost but the basis for the **Synoptic Gospels**

Q-Source: Theoretical source for material common to **Matthew** and **Luke** that is not shared by **Mark**; from German *Quelle* ('source')

Redaction Criticism: Interpretation of the Bible based on the idea of a redactor editing earlier material to address issues going on in the church in his time

***Sitz im Leben*:** 'Life Situation'; the context in which the *pericopae* were first composed, according to **Form Criticism**, or edited into their current form according to **Redaction Criticism**

Source Criticism: Interpretation of the Bible based on the different sources each Gospel is composed of

Synoptic Gospel: Matthew, Mark and **Luke**; from the Greek 'seen together' because of the shared content and structure of these Gospels

3.1 INTERPRETING THE TEXT

Jesus wrote no books: everything we know was written after his Crucifixion (33 CE); earliest Christian documents = **epistles** (letters) of **Paul** (50s CE); Paul mentions that Jesus was betrayed and crucified, had twelve Disciples, refers to meeting **Peter** (calls him 'Cephas')

Gospels: biographies of Jesus written when the Christians who had known Jesus started to die.

- **Mark's Gospel (68-70 CE, Rome?):** earliest Gospel (**Markan Priority**); attributed to Peter's secretary in Rome; poor standard of Greek; author doesn't seem to know about destruction of Jerusalem Temple (70 CE); explains Jewish customs for Gentile readers

- **Matthew's Gospel (c.85 CE, Antioch?):** once thought to be earliest Gospel; very 'Jewish' Gospel: does not explain Jewish customs; uses **proof-texts** from the Old Testament; good knowledge of 1st century Palestine; supposed to be written by Matthew Levi, publican who joined Jesus' Disciples

- **Luke's Gospel (c.85 CE, Greece?):** last of the Synoptic Gospels to be written; a report gathered from eyewitnesses; good standard of Greek for an educated audience but only hazy understanding of 1st century Palestine; some specific details of the Roman siege of Jerusalem in 70 CE; focus on Gentiles and Jesus' ethical teachings; the 'Gospel of Compassion'; focus on salvation for all

- **John's Gospel (90-100 CE, Ephesus?):** last Gospel to be written; describes Jesus' enemies as "*the Jews*"; 'high Christology' (Jesus is **Word of God made Flesh**); refers to Christians being expelled from Synagogues (80s-90s CE); 'backward-looking' style; more accurate knowledge of pre-70 CE Jerusalem than other Gospels so might go back to original eyewitnesses.

Oral tradition: stories about Jesus circulating among Christians before they were written down; might have deviated from the historical facts:

- **Catholic/Conservative Protestant:** Oral tradition faithfully preserved Jesus' historic behaviour, words and teachings

- **Liberal/Modernist scholars**: Oral tradition distorted Jesus' behaviour, words and teachings, attributing to Jesus things that actually reflect later Christian ideas & Christologies

Christology: belief about Jesus' status: human teacher, inspired prophet, supernatural wonderworker, angelic being or God-in-human-form?

- **Low Christology:** Jesus is a human being EXALTED (raised up, promoted) by God to a supernatural state; perhaps the earliest Christian belief

- **High Christology:** Jesus is a divine being INCARNATED in human form; perhaps a belief Christians developed later in 1st century

3.1 THE SYNOPTIC PROBLEM

'Synoptic' = 'seen together': passages from Synoptic Gospels (Matthew, Mark, Luke) are similar. Sometimes word-for-word the same

Shared Wording: Synoptics share 50% of same words but only 10% with **John**; **Matthew** & **Mark** share 90% introducing John the Baptst

- **Example Feeding 5000:** in all 4 Gospels; Synoptics say *"taking 5 loaves and two fish"* (*ichthus* for 'fish'), *"looking up into heaven he blessed them"*, *"all ate and were satisfied"*; **John** has different phrases and *opsarion* for 'fish' (= kippers)

Parenthetical material: = 'in brackets'; usually identical; feature of writing not speech, so can't be explained by all being eyewitnesses

- **Example:** *(Let the reader understand)*: **Mark** & **Matthew** both use this when describing Jesus' prediction of the Apocalypse (end of the world); addressed to a reader yet identical in both

Luke's Prologue: admits using material from earlier sources

- **Example:** *"just as they were handed down to us by those who from the first were eyewitnesses"*: uses sources, not an eyewitness

Solutions to Synoptic Problem	Strength	Criticism
Gospels are independent eyewitness	Fits with traditional authors who were actual Disciples (**Matthew, John**) or friends of Disciples (**Mark, Luke**)	Synoptic similarities become a problem – clear evidence of copying from each other
Inspiration by Holy Spirit	Fits with idea of Scripture being divinely inspired and wording being precisely influenced by God	Does not explain synoptic differences or why **John** is so dissimilar
Proto-Gospel	Missing original Gospel (*ur*-Gospel) that all others are taken from (e.g. written by **Peter** or **Thomas**)	No evidence for this text; never mentioned by early Christian writers (e.g. **Irenaeus**)
Multiple sources	The Gospels borrow from each other and from earlier sources now lost (e.g. **Q-Source**)	No mention of these earlier sources by early Christian writers, who describe **Matthew** as first Gospel

Despite its criticisms, 'multiple sources' is the most popular solution to the Synoptic Problem today

3.1 SOLUTIONS TO THE SYNOPTIC PROBLEM

PROTO-GOSPEL

Theory: Original Gospel, written in Aramaic (Jesus' language), perhaps had a Greek translation; just sayings (*logia*) of Jesus with no stories; original preaching (*kerygma*) of Jesus and his Disciples before it was altered by later Christians

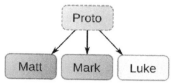

Proto-Mark: early version of **Mark** behind current **Mark, Matthew** & **Luke**

Gospel of Thomas: discovered in 4th century BCE but may go back to 1st century; consists entirely of *logia* (sayings), 50% shared with Synoptics

Criticisms: Irenaeus (180 CE) only mentions **Matthew, Mark, Luke, John** (= the *Tetramorph*); no evidence for **proto-Mark** or version of **Thomas** this early

MARKAN PRIORITY

Theory: Mark misses out popular Christian material (Virgin Birth, Lord's Prayer) which Mt/Lk add; has bad Greek or mistakes that Mt/Lk correct; uses Aramaic expression (e.g. *corban*) that Mt/Lk remove; contains 'hard readings' (e.g. angry Jesus) that Mt/Lk remove or explain

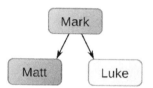

Criticism: goes against earliest writers who thought **Matthew** the first Gospel; doesn't explain where material comes from that Mt/Lk share but which *isn't* in Mark

Q-SOURCE: 2-SOURCE SOLUTION (2SS)

Theory: Matthew & Luke are based on **Mark** plus a source ('*Q*') that they share but Mark doesn't use; *Q* contains *logia* (e.g. love your enemies) and some Parables; explains why Mt/Lk resemble Mark and why they also contain similar material that *isn't* in Mark

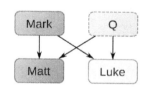

Criticism: no physical evidence for '*Q*' and '*Q*' is never mentioned by earliest Christian writers; doesn't explain material shared by Mt/Lk that isn't in Mark

Q-SOURCE: 4-SOURCE SOLUTION (4SS)

Theory: Matthew & Luke are based on **Mark** plus '*Q*' but each also has its own source (**M** and **L**) that other doesn't use; better theory than 2SS → explains differences between Matthew & Luke *as well as* similarities

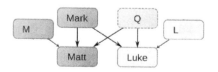

Criticism: proposes 3 sources never mentioned by ancient writers and no physical copies – principle of parsimony (Occam's Razor) says simpler explanations are better → e.g. '2-Gospel Hypothesis' that **Matthew & Luke** were written first and **Mark** was based on them both

3.1 BIBLICAL CRITICISM

SOURCE CRITICISM

Theory: Gospels are not eyewitness accounts but blends of 'sources' (written or oral traditions); tries to identify original sources and what they were like; ignores **revelation** or the Holy Spirit *'inspiring'* writers; does not treat Bible as inerrant (without mistakes) - it *looks* for mistakes which show material from different sources (e.g. **Mark** incorrectly refers to Herod Antipas as "king" but **Luke/Matthew** correct this to "*tetrarch*")

Example: Synoptic Problem and various solutions

Implications: Source Criticism has secular (non-religious) assumptions: Bible is a collection of human documents, not divinely inspired ones; contains errors and contradictions; assembled through copying and editing earlier sources; Gospels not eyewitnesses; prophecies (e.g. destruction of Jerusalem in 70 CE) written in hindsight

FORM CRITICISM

Theory: Gospels are made up of **"units"** (*pericopae*) passed down as **oral (word-of-mouth) tradition**; tries to identify these 'units' and work out what they *originally* meant; **Hermann Gunkel** (1918) used "*Sitz im Leben*" ("setting in life") to refer to social context that a *pericope* was created in

Examples: Martin Dibelius (1919): (1) **Paradigms** (stories presenting Jesus as a role model, e.g. Jesus' crucifixion); (2) **Tales** (miracle stories meant to entertain); (3) **Myths** (non-historical, e.g. Devil tempting Jesus); (4) **Legends** (seem to be historical but heroic fiction, e.g. **birth-narratives**); **Exhortations** (wise sayings, e.g. *love your enemy*)

Implications: Bible contains different genres (e.g. **John's Prologue** may have started as a hymn); Gospels largely fictional or exaggerated; no possibility of reconstructing the 'historical Jesus'; Christian beliefs don't go back to Jesus himself; **Rudolf Bultmann** argues Gospels must be **de-mythologized** to appeal to modern people

REDACTION CRITICISM

Theory: Gospel-writers are editors or **REDACTORS** of their material; they **choose, edit and alter the texts** to suit their own agenda; focus on distinctive vocabulary and recurring **MOTIFS** (e.g. **"I am" statements, proof-texts**); compare different Gospels' accounts of same event and focus on differences revealing redactor's purposes (e.g. **John** never names Jesus' mother because Jesus' human background is unimportant to his 'high Christological' beliefs)

Example: John's use the phrase "*the Jews*" to describe Jesus' reveals the antisemitic agenda of the Johannine Community, rooted in their own experience of being cast out of the Synagogues

Implications: emphasizes creativity of Gospel-writers; emphasizes importance of the social setting (*Sitz im Leben)* of redactors; turns the Gospels into propaganda writing; Gospels not "*inspired*" and not eyewitnesses: more like modern journalism with bias.

3.2 AUTHORSHIP OF FOURTH GOSPEL

Fourth Gospel = **John's Gospel**

JOHN SON OF ZEBEDEE

Traditional author, youngest of Twelve Disciples, he and brother James were Galilean fishermen, followers of John the Baptist who left to follow Jesus; died in 98 CE in Ephesus (Turkey)

In favour of John son of Zebedee	Against John son of Zebedee
Ephesus in late 1st century CE is right time, right place; 3 epistles (letters) by 'John' have similar themes/language; early church traditions claim John is the author; **John Robinson** (1984) argues John wrote Fourth Gospel in 60s CE and is *"the other disciple"* who is witness at Jesus' trial	Fourth Gospel never claims to be by 'John', epistles may be by different Johns (common name); Galilean peasant fisherman couldn't write such good Greek or know Hellenic philosophy (*Logos*, etc)

BELOVED DISCIPLE

Mysterious figure in final chapters of Gospel: "*the disciple whom Jesus loved*" or "*the beloved disciple of Jesus*"; appears 5 times: at Jesus' farewell Discourse, at the foot of the Cross, at the Empty Tomb and 2 times when the Risen Christ appears to the other Disciples; Fourth Gospel ends claiming that the Beloved Disciple wrote the Gospel:

> *This is the disciple who testifies to these things and who wrote them down. We know that his testimony is true* - **John 21: 24**

- **Beloved Disciple is John son of Zebedee:** view of several early Christian writers; John son of Zebedee absent in Fourth Gospel; BUT BD only appears in **John 13**, whereas John son of Zebedee was a Disciple right from the beginning.

- **BD is Lazarus:** The BD only appears after **Lazarus has been raised from the dead**. Lazarus is three times described as the person Jesus "*loved*"

- **BD is symbolic:** The BD represents believing Christians generally - or the reader

JOHANNINE COMMUNITY

Raymond E. Brown proposes that Fourth Gospel was a community effort, written in stages, not complete until 100 CE; originally followers of John the Baptist; Jewish Christians thrown out of the Synagogue c.90 CE; Gospel doesn't just report the life and Resurrection of Jesus: it's also an **allegory** for the experiences of the Johannine Community itself

Johannine Community regarded BD as its founder; its us-vs-them attitude shown in its hostility to Jews and Christian churches founded by Peter (BD is always shown as better than Peter); developed 'high Christology' compared to other Christian groups

3.2 PURPOSES OF FOURTH GOSPEL

these are written that you may believe that Jesus is the Christ, the Son of God, and that by believing you may have life in his name - **John 20: 31**

JESUS AS 'CHRIST'

Christos is Greek word for '**Messiah**'; in Synoptics, Jesus is secretive about being the Messiah, but in John's Gospel he announces it openly (e.g. Andrew tells Peter: *We have found the Messiah* - **John 1: 41**)

C.H. Dodd argues most important meaning of 'Christ' is a **King**; Nathanael calls Jesus "*King of Israel*" at start and Pontius Pilate mocks him as "*Jesus of Nazareth, King of the Jews*" at the end.

Fourth Gospel never mentions **line of David**, rejects **Kingly Messiah**: after the **Feeding of the 5000** the they try to crown Jesus king, but he escapes; Jesus tells Pilate *My kingdom is not of this world* (**John 18: 36**) → Christ is a spiritual King who rules over souls, not an earthly king who rules over territory

C.H. Dodd argues that 'Christ' = the **'Lamb of God'**; John the Baptist recognises Jesus as: *the Lamb of God, who takes away the sin of the world!* - **John 1: 29**

Dodd and **Raymond E. Brown** conclude phrase is not something John the Baptist actually said (it's not in Synoptics); link to **Paschal Lamb** → Jesus dying on the Cross at same time as Paschal Lamb sacrificed in Temple for Passover: Jesus is TRUE Lamb of God, TRUE sacrifice→ different from Jewish view of Messiah, distinctively Johannine view of Jesus as the Christ.

JESUS AS 'SON OF GOD'

Huios Theos = Greek for '**Son of God**': 29 times in **John**; God as 'Father' over 100 times in **John**

Old Testament: SoG can mean whole Jewish nation or king of Israel (symbolic); **Synoptics:** similar to Jewish view (**Mark**, Jesus is 'adopted' as SoG when baptized; **Matthew** and **Luke** Jesus is announced to be SoG when conceived)

The Fourth Gospel: High Christology: Jesus is SoG since the creation of the universe; eternal being who is now present on Earth; he remembers his pre-existence:

I know where I came from and where I am going - **John 8: 14**

Before Abraham was, I am! - **John 8: 58**

C.H. Dodd argues Jesus is on a journey God → Earth then Earth → God again – taking with him those who **believe in him** by drawing them into his spiritual world of **Eternal Life**.

'LIFE IN HIS NAME'

> *to those who believed in his name, he gave the right to become children of God* - **John 1: 12**

Life = zoë-Life: eternal, timeless, fulfilled living in the here-and-now received by **believing in Jesus** (personal transformation, being 'Born Again')

In his Name = because Jesus is SoG, his name = God's Name → Jesus has God's authority → act in Jesus' Name, you receive Jesus' status and his *Zoe*-life → means living like Jesus: a life of selflessness, compassionate love and sacrifice for others

> *If you love me, keep my commands, I will ask the Father, and he will give you another Paraclete to help you and be with you for ever* - **John 14: 15-1**

Paraclete = 'Helper' → the **Holy Spirit,** which is the power of God: guiding, strengthening, answering their prayers → EVANGELICAL churches emphasise religious experiences, being **'Born Again'**, Gifts of the Spirit show that Christians are **living in Jesus' Name**

> **C.H. Dodd:** REALISED ESCHATOLOGY is idea that **Eternal** Life is enjoyed in the present rather than the Afterlife: a changed way of living, full of joy and love

A 'SPIRITUAL GOSPEL'

Clement of Alexandria (150-215 CE): *John, aware that the physical facts had been set out in the Gospels... composed a spiritual Gospel*

Flesh and Spirit: Synoptics describe physical facts vs John's deeper meaning behind; Synoptics are DESCRIPTIVE but John is REFLECTIVE; Synoptics record *IPSISSIMA VERBA* (true words) of Jesus but John captures *IPSISSIMA VOX* (the true voice)

GREAT

QUOTE

> *The Gospel of John is like a swimming pool: shallow enough that a child may wade and deep enough that an elephant can swim* **– Leon Morris**

Symbolism makes John most Christians' favourite Gospel but interpretation leads to problems:

Gnostic Heresy: 2nd century Johannine churches split between Christians and **Gnostics** who believed a secret code (in Greek, *gnosis*) in Fourth Gospel, believed spiritual realities = all-important, physical world = evil → Jesus = spirit-being who only ***appeared*** to be human

> **Raymond E. Brown** calls these Gnostics "secessionists" ('splitters' who broke from church's teachings); their beliefs "*a plausible exaggeration... of certain features of the Fourth Gospel*" → took symbols of being Born Again and receiving **Eternal Life** to extreme conclusion; 3 later **epistles** (letters) by 'John' condemn these splitters

FULFILMENT OF SCRIPTURE

Suffering Servant (Isaiah 53): dies in the place of his people → High Priest Caiaphas justifies killing Jesus so that *"one man dies for the people"* (**John 11: 50**); SS tortured by the very people he tries to help:

> *He came to that which was his own, but his own did not receive him* - **John 1: 11**

Crucifixion: shows prophecies being fulfilled:

	a pack of villains encircles me; they pierce my hands and my feet - **Psalm 22: 16**	Jesus crucified between two thieves
	They divide my clothes among them and cast lots for my garment - **Psalm 22: 18**	Jesus' clothes are shared between his executioners; soldiers throw dice to see who gets his robe
	They will look on me, the one they have pierced, and they will mourn for him as one mourns for an only child - **Zechariah 12: 10**	A soldier checks Jesus is dead by stabbing him with a spear while Jesus' mother watches on

A GOSPEL TO CONVERT JEWS & GENTILES

MISSIONARY RELIGION (convert others); the **'Great Commission'** in **Matthew 28: 19**; version appears at end of **Fourth Gospel**:

> *As the Father has sent me, so I send you* - **John 20: 21**

Converting Jews: Gospel starts with imitation of the **Book of Genesis** (*"in the beginning..."*); Andrew tells Peter: "*We have found the Messiah*"; Jesus corrects Jewish beliefs about God and the **Law**; identifies specific places in Jerusalem (eg Pool of Siloam); Jesus' actions often correspond to Jewish festivals

- **Criticisms:** "*the Jews*" are represented as evil: *children of the Devil* (**John 8: 44**); 'high Christology' seen as blasphemous to many Jews

Converting Gentiles: presents Jesus in **Hellenic** terms (e.g. the **Logos**); universal symbolism of **light and darkness, flesh and spirit**, bread, water and birth; **Jesus as the Son of God** not blasphemous to pagans; offers **Eternal Life** without complicated rituals or circumcision

- **Criticisms:** Gentiles don't feature much in this Gospel; Jesus spends most of his time arguing with Jewish leaders; specific details about Jerusalem and Jewish festivals confusing for Gentiles

> **Raymond E. Brown** believes Johannine Community wrote the Fourth Gospel to appeal to *"crypto-Christians"* in the Jewish community who concealed their faith in Jesus.

TOPIC 3 EXAM QUESTIONS & REVISION ACTIVITIES

AS-Level Paper 3 (New Testament)

Section A

1   Explore the key ideas concerning the authorship of the Fourth Gospel. (9 marks)

2   Assess the significance of Form Criticism in interpreting the New Testament text. (9 marks)

3   Assess the strengths of the idea of the 'Q source' to explain the relationship between the synoptic Gospels. (9 marks)

Section B

4   (a) Explore **two** key ideas about the purposes of the Fourth Gospel: Jesus as Christ, Jesus as Son of God, life in his name, a spiritual Gospel. (8 marks)

   (b) Analyse the view that the Fourth Gospel's purpose is to convert Jews & Gentiles. (20 marks)

Total = 54 marks

A-Level Paper 3 (New Testament)

Section A

1   Explore the key ideas of Form Criticism. (8 marks)

2   Assess the view that the four-source solution explains the relationship between the synoptic Gospels. (12 marks)

Section B

Read the following passage before answering the questions.

> [41] At this the Jews there began to grumble about him because he said, "I am the bread that came down from heaven." [42] They said, "Is this not Jesus, the son of Joseph, whose father and mother we know? How can he now say, 'I came down from heaven'?"

[43] "Stop grumbling among yourselves," Jesus answered. [44] "No one can come to me unless the Father who sent me draws them, and I will raise them up at the last day. [45] It is written in the Prophets: 'They will all be taught by God.' Everyone who has heard the Father and learned from him comes to me. [46] No one has seen the Father except the one who is from God; only he has seen the Father. [47] Very truly I tell you, the one who believes has eternal life. [48] I am the bread of life. [49] Your ancestors ate the manna in the wilderness, yet they died. [50] But here is the bread that comes down from heaven, which anyone may eat and not die. [51] I am the living bread that came down from heaven. Whoever eats this bread will live forever. This bread is my flesh, which I will give for the life of the world."

[52] Then the Jews began to argue sharply among themselves, "How can this man give us his flesh to eat?"

[53] Jesus said to them, "Very truly I tell you, unless you eat the flesh of the Son of Man and drink his blood, you have no life in you. [54] Whoever eats my flesh and drinks my blood has eternal life, and I will raise them up at the last day...."

Quote from New International Translation, John 6: 41-54

3   (a) Clarify the ideas illustrated in this passage about the purposes of the Fourth Gospel as expressed in this passage. *You must refer to the passage in your response.* (10 marks)

(b) Assess the claim that the Fourth Gospel was written to reveal the identity of Jesus. (20 marks)

Section C

4   Evaluate the view that we cannot reconstruct the historical Jesus from studying the New Testament text.

Evaluate this view in the context of the interpretation of the text. In your response to this question, you must include how developments in New Testament Studies have been influenced by one of the following:

- Philosophy of Religion

- Religion and Ethics

- the study of a religion.

(30 marks)

Total = 90 marks

In these example papers, all the questions are drawn from Topic 3 (although the Anthology passage is from Topic 2, since there's no Anthology extract linked to Topic 3). A real exam would not be like this and each question would probably draw from a different Topic instead.

Comprehension Quiz

1   What is meant by the Synoptic Problem?

2   Given an example of a similarity across the Synoptic Gospels

3   What is a proto-Gospel?

4   What is the Q source?

5   Explain the 4-source solution (4SS).

6   What is 'Sitz Im Leben'?

7   What is a pericope?

8   What is a redactor?

9   In what way is Wrede's theory of the Messianic Secret an example of Redaction Criticism?

10   Who was John son of Zebedee?

11   What is the Johannine Community?

12   In what sense is Jesus the 'Lamb of God'?

13   What is meant by a 'high' Christology?

14   Give three ways that the circumstances of Jesus' death fulfill the Scriptures.

15   Who were the 'crypto-Christians'?

Bible Quotes to match

Explain how each quote links to this Topic

1   *He came to that which was his own, but his own did not receive him* – **John 1: 11**

2   *these are written that you may believe that Jesus is the Christ, the Son of God, and that by believing you may have life in his name* – **John 20: 31**

3   *"Before Abraham was, I am!"* – **John 8: 58**

4   *a pack of villains encircles me; they pierce my hands and my feet* – **Psalm 22: 16**

5   *"As the Father has sent me, so I send you"* – **John 20: 21**

6   *" If you love me, keep my commands, I will ask the Father, and he will give you another Paraclete to help you and be with you for ever"* – **John 14: 15-1**

7   *"We have found the Messiah"* – **John 1: 41**

8   *The Gospel of John is like a swimming pool: shallow enough that a child may wade and deep enough that an elephant can swim* – **Leon Morris** (not a Bible quote but worth knowing)

Word Search

Find 20 terms/names from this Topic and explain them (NB. 'Q' isn't one of them)

```
E Y L D N E G E L T C B S R X
L L E P S O G O T O R P G M R
L D P Y R C I A M A R A K X P
E C S I S E H T N E R A P W A
U Y O D C C D S A M Q J P D R
Q U G R B S I A J T Z N O E A
F P L G B U I T C Z R G H U C
N E A K K A U D P T F O W O L
L R U D K I N I D O I K H I E
S I T Z I M L E B E N O Q X T
K C I I G G R M D C V Y N V E
R O R P A R A D I G M O S H P
X P I Z A L P G E N T I L E N
V E P A S C H A L L A M B E T
V T S I R H C V A C D C B S B
```

Crossword

Across

3. Textual unit in Form Criticism
6. _____ Disciple, possible author of the Fourth Gospel
10. _____ Lamb, sacrificed for Passover
11. Traditionally believed to be the first Gospel
12. The earliest Gospel, according to most scholars
13. ____ Im Leben
14. Language Jesus spoke

Down

1. German for 'source'
2. Key scholar who proposed Fourth Gospel was written to convert crypto-Christians
4. Heretics who interpreted Fourth Gospel as a spiritual code
5. Matthew, Mark & Luke
7. Famous Form Critic
8. Called John's Gospel a 'Spiritual Gospel'
9. Editor of a Gospel
10. Helper or Advocate

Debates in this Topic

Indicate where you stand on this debate by marking a cross on the line then list points in favour and points against your position (more in favour the closer to the edge, more against the closer to the middle)

The Gospels are eyewitness accounts of the events they describe

The Gospels consist of material that is legendary or fictional

John's Gospel was written by one of Jesus' own disciples

The Fourth Gospel has unique themes

The purpose of the Fourth Gospel is to convert Jews and Gentiles

Cloze Exercise

Traditionally, Christians believed the Gospels to be _____accounts of Jesus' ministry. _____and John are supposed to be by actual Disciples of Jesus and Luke and _____by people who knew the Disciples personally. However, modern scholarship casts doubt on this.

_____Criticism explores the idea that the Gospels are created from pre-existing sources, such as earlier books or _____(spoken) traditions. This is a solution to the_____, which is the recognition that Matthew, Mark and _____share too much exact text to be completely independent of each other. One possibility is a_____, like an early version of Matthew or Mark that the others copied. Some scholars suggest that the Gospel of _____could be this missing source.

Another theory is that a lost source known as 'Q' (from the German word for 'source', "_____") lies behind Matthew and Luke, who otherwise borrow from Mark, which is the earliest Gospel. In the 4-Source _____(4SS), Matthew and Luke have their own sources and also mix Mark and 'Q' in different ways. However, arguing against this is the fact that the earliest Christian writers such as _____all declare Matthew to be the oldest Gospel and never mention 'Q' or any other earlier source.

_____Criticism argues that the Gospels were composed like _____puzzles from textual units called_____. These units circulated in the early churches as unwritten traditions about Jesus. _____categorizes them as _____that show Jesus as a role model or fantastical _____that are only meant to entertain. These critics cast doubt on whether the Gospels tell us anything about the _____Jesus.

_____Criticism argues that the Gospels were written by editors who took previous material and altered it to suit their own agendas. For example, Matthew portrays Jesus as the 'new_____' and John has a strong anti-Jewish bias. Also, Gospels like Mark have a _____Christology presenting Jesus as human but John has a _____Christology, presenting Jesus as a divine being.

There are different theories about the authorship of John's Gospel. Tradition claims it was written by John son of_____, the youngest of Jesus' Disciples. However, the sophisticated language makes this unlikely. The character of the '_____' who appears at the end of the Gospel may represent the author. Others argue the Gospel was composed by the_____, a group of Jewish Christians who were expelled from their _____ around 90 CE because of their beliefs about Jesus.

John's Gospel has distinctive beliefs, such as Jesus being the '_____' who dies as a sacrifice, and the importance of being 'Born Again' rather than following the Jewish Law. _____thinks it was aimed at _____ who remained behind in the Synagogues and needed encouraging to declare themselves as believers in Christ.

Beloved Disciple, Brown, crypto-Christians, Dibelius, eyewitness, Form, high, historical, Irenaeus, jigsaw, Johannine Community, Lamb of God' , Luke, low, Mark , Matthew, Moses, oral, paradigms, pericopae, proto-Gospel, Quelle, Redaction, Solution, Source, Synagogues, Synoptic Problem, tales, Thomas, Zebedee

EXAM PRACTICE PAPERS

AS-Level Paper 3 (New Testament)

Section A

1 Explore the key ideas concerning the line of David. (9 marks)

2 Assess the significance of the Sign of raising Lazarus from the dead in the Fourth Gospel. (9 marks)

3 Assess the arguments for the authorship of the Fourth Gospel. (9 marks)

Section B

4 (a) Explore **two** titles of Jesus in the Synoptic Gospels. (8 marks)

   (b) Analyse the view that Jesus' identity cannot be understood without reference to the Old Testament. (20 marks)

Total = 54 marks

A-Level Paper 3 (New Testament)

Section A

1 Explore the key ideas about the purposes of the Fourth Gospel. (8 marks)

2 Assess the view that the Gospels have been redacted to reflect the concerns of 1st century Christians. (12 marks)

Section B

Read the following passage before answering the questions.

The Word Became Flesh

[1] In the beginning was the Word, and the Word was with God, and the Word was God. [2] He was with God in the beginning. [3] Through him all things were made; without him nothing was made that has been made. [4] In him was life, and that life was the light of all mankind. [5] The light shines in the darkness, and the darkness has not overcome it.

[6] There was a man sent from God whose name was John. [7] He came as a witness to testify concerning that light, so that through him all might believe. [8] He himself was not the light; he came only as a witness to the light.

[9] The true light that gives light to everyone was coming into the world. [10] He was in the world, and though the world was made through him, the world did not recognize him. [11] He came to that which was his own, but his own did not receive him. [12] Yet to all who did receive him, to those who believed in his name, he gave the right to become children of God – [13] children born not of natural descent, nor of human decision or a husband's will, but born of God.

[14] The Word became flesh and made his dwelling among us. We have seen his glory, the glory of the one and only Son, who came from the Father, full of grace and truth.

Quote from New International Translation, John 1: 1-14

3   (a) Clarify the ideas illustrated in this passage about the person of Jesus as expressed in this passage. *You must refer to the passage in your response.* (10 marks)

       (b) Assess implication for religious laws and codes for living of different understandings of the identity Jesus, including its influence beyond a religious community. (20 marks)

Section C

4   Evaluate the view that we cannot understand the identity and message of Jesus without understanding the historical context of the New Testament.

       Evaluate this view in the context of the world of the 1st century. In your response to this question, you must include how developments in New Testament Studies have been influenced by one of the following:

- Philosophy of Religion

- Religion and Ethics

- the study of a religion.

(30 marks)

Total = 90 marks

In these example papers, all the questions are drawn from Topics 1-3 This is correct for the AS exam but a real A-Level exam would draw from Topics 4-6 as well.

ABOUT THE AUTHOR

Jonathan Rowe is a teacher of Religious Studies, Psychology and Sociology at Spalding Grammar School and he creates and maintains **www.philosophydungeon.weebly.com** for Edexcel evelReligious Studies and **www.psychologywizard.net** site for Edexcel A-Level Psychology. He has worked as an examiner for various Exam Boards but is not affiliated with Edexcel. This series of books grew out of the resources he created for his students. Jonathan also writes novels and creates resources for his hobby of fantasy wargaming. He likes warm beer and smooth jazz.

Printed in Great Britain
by Amazon